T0129472

Understanding Human Evolution

Human life, and how we came to be, is one of the greatest scientific and philosophical questions of our time. This compact and accessible book presents a modern view of human evolution. Written by a leading authority, it lucidly and engagingly explains not only the evolutionary process, but the technologies currently used to unravel the evolutionary past and emergence of *Homo sapiens*. By separating the history of paleoanthropology from current interpretation of the human fossil record, it lays numerous misconceptions to rest, and demonstrates that human evolution has been far from the linear struggle from primitiveness to perfection that we've been led to believe. It also presents a coherent scenario for how *Homo sapiens* contrived to cross a formidable cognitive barrier to become an extraordinary and unprecedented thinking creature. Elegantly illustrated, *Understanding Human Evolution* is for anyone interested in the complex and tangled story of how we came to be.

Ian Tattersall is Curator Emeritus in the Division of Anthropology of the American Museum of Natural History, New York, USA. With around 400 papers and 30 books published in primatology and evolutionary biology, he has received prizes from organizations ranging from the American Association of Physical Anthropologists to the Accademia Lincei of Rome and the Monuments Conservancy. He has conducted fieldwork in countries as diverse as Madagascar, Yemen, Vietnam, and Mauritius.

The **Understanding Life** series is for anyone wanting an engaging and concise way into a key biological topic. Offering a multidisciplinary perspective, these accessible guides address common misconceptions and misunderstandings in a thoughtful way to help stimulate debate and encourage a more in-depth understanding. Written by leading thinkers in each field, these books are for anyone wanting an expert overview that will enable clearer thinking on each topic.

Series Editor: Kostas Kampourakis http://kampourakis.com

Published titles:

Understanding Evolution	Kostas Kampourakis	9781108746083
Understanding Coronavirus	Raul Rabadan	9781108826716
Understanding Development	Alessandro Minelli	9781108799232
Understanding Evo-Devo	Wallace Arthur	9781108819466
Understanding Genes	Kostas Kampourakis	9781108812825
Understanding DNA Ancestry	Sheldon Krimsky	9781108816038
Understanding Intelligence	Ken Richardson	9781108940368
Understanding Metaphors in the Life Sciences	Andrew S. Reynolds	9781108940498
Understanding Cancer	Robin Hesketh	9781009005999
Understanding How Science Explains the World	Kevin McCain	9781108995504
Understanding Race	Rob DeSalle and Ian Tattersall	9781009055581
Understanding Human Evolution	Ian Tattersall	9781009101998

Forthcoming:

Understanding Human Metabolism	Keith N. Frayn	9781009108522
Understanding Fertility	Gab Kovacs	9781009054164
Understanding Forensic DNA	Suzanne Bell and John M. Butler	9781009044011
Understanding Natural Selection	Michael Ruse	9781009088329
Understanding Creationism	Glenn Branch	9781108927505
Understanding Species	John S. Wilkins	9781108987196
Understanding the Nature–Nurture Debate	Eric Turkheimer	9781108958165

Understanding Human Evolution

IAN TATTERSALL
American Museum of Natural History, New York

CAMBRIDGE
UNIVERSITY PRESS

CAMBRIDGE
UNIVERSITY PRESS

Shaftesbury Road, Cambridge CB2 8EA, United Kingdom

One Liberty Plaza, 20th Floor, New York, NY 10006, USA

477 Williamstown Road, Port Melbourne, VIC 3207, Australia

314–321, 3rd Floor, Plot 3, Splendor Forum, Jasola District Centre, New Delhi – 110025, India

103 Penang Road, #05–06/07, Visioncrest Commercial, Singapore 238467

Cambridge University Press is part of Cambridge University Press & Assessment, a department of the University of Cambridge.

We share the University's mission to contribute to society through the pursuit of education, learning and research at the highest international levels of excellence.

www.cambridge.org
Information on this title: www.cambridge.org/9781009101998

DOI: 10.1017/9781009106177

First published 2022

A catalogue record for this publication is available from the British Library

ISBN   978-1-009-09875-5   Hardback
ISBN   978-1-009-10199-8   Paperback

"For years, Ian Tattersall has been *the* go-to source for the latest facts and interpretations of human evolution. Here, in his clear, pithy style, he brings us up to date on the latest discoveries, weaving them skillfully into a coherent outline of hominid history extending back millions of years. It's all here – from the latest on DNA and radiometric dating of fossils, to the nature and origin of the still-mysterious self-consciousness that is unique to modern humans. A terrific resource and wonderful read!"

Niles Eldredge, Curator Emeritus in the Division of Paleontology, American Museum of Natural History, USA

"Ian Tattersall provides in this short and engaging book the story of how humans evolved, and, as importantly, how we have come to learn about our evolutionary history and the nature of being human through great discoveries and great scientific debates."

Robert Foley, Leverhulme Professor of Human Evolution, University of Cambridge, UK

"*Understanding Human Evolution* provides a sweeping overview of the field of human evolution, giving equal attention to the history of the discipline as well as current thoughts and ideas about our attainment of the milestones of human evolution – upright posture and bipedal locomotion, the evolution of tool use, the expansion of the brain and human cognition, the development of language, and the spread of humans out of Africa around the globe. All of this is presented in a concise and accessible package by one of the most well-known popularizers of the field today. This is an excellent resource for anyone looking for an introduction to the fossil evidence for human evolution, as well as those who want to catch up on the current state of knowledge in this fast-moving discipline."

Leslie C. Aiello FBA, Professor Emerita, University College London, UK

"An enjoyable, highly informative, and scholarly read. Tattersall is at his best here. Engaging the reader with his inimitable style, he interprets and explains the convoluted evidence for how we became human. Written largely for the non-specialist, there is much here that will inform and even stimulate professional paleoanthropologists."

Donald Johanson, Founding Director of the Institute of Human Origins at Arizona State University, USA

To the memory of
Jakov Radovčić (1946–2021)
Paleontologist, Curator, Friend

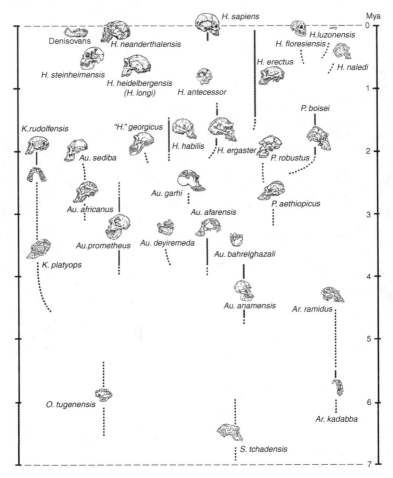

Distribution of fossil hominin species in time, showing how several different species typically coexisted prior to the arrival of *Homo sapiens*. Dotted lines are indications of depth of lineage, and not indicators of relationship.

Contents

Maps

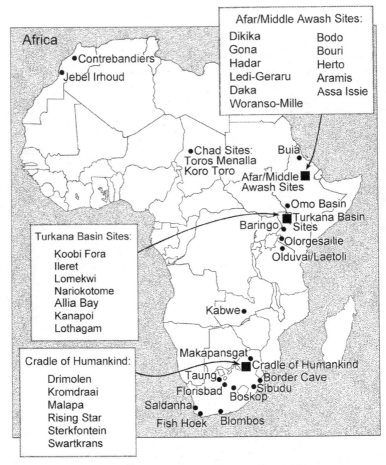

Afar/Middle Awash Sites:

Dikika   Bodo
Gona   Bouri
Hadar   Herto
Ledi-Geraru   Aramis
Daka   Assa Issie
Woranso-Mille

Africa

●Contrebandiers

●Jebel Irhoud

●Chad Sites:
Toros Menalla
Koro Toro

Buia

Afar/Middle ■
Awash Sites

Omo Basin

Turkana Basin ■ Turkana Basin
Baringo●   Sites

●Olorgesailie

Olduvai/Laetoli

Turkana Basin Sites:

Koobi Fora
Ileret
Lomekwi
Nariokotome
Allia Bay
Kanapoi
Lothagam

Kabwe●

Makapansgat

Cradle of Humankind ■ Cradle of Humankind

Taung●   ●Border Cave

Cradle of Humankind:

Drimolen
Kromdraai
Malapa
Rising Star
Sterkfontein
Swartkrans

Florisbad●   ●Sibudu
        Boskop

Saldanha●

Fish Hoek   Blombos

Map 1 The major African hominin fossil sites mentioned in this book.

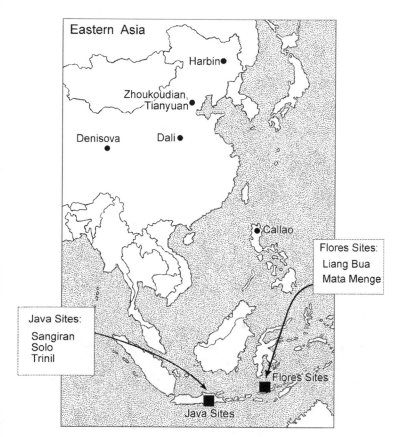

Map 2 The major Asian hominin fossil sites mentioned in this book.

Map 3   The major European hominin fossil sites mentioned in this book.

Foreword

Who are we, where do we come from, and how have we come to be what we are? These are questions that have been puzzling humans for thousands of years, at least since the first written evidence of philosophical and metaphysical reflections. It is very well known that different kinds of answers have been given to these questions over the years from various scholarly, and not so scholarly, domains. However, what do the biological sciences, and especially paleoanthropology – the study of human evolution – have to say about these questions? In this splendid book, Ian Tattersall provides an amazingly rich account of what we have come to know during the last 200 years or so about human evolution – not only about the evolution of our own species, *Homo sapiens*, during the last 200,000 years, but also of other hominin species. As the author explains, there is so much evidence from several independent sources that has established human evolution as a fact of life. There is thus no question that we have common ancestors with the apes, from which our ancestors diverged over the last few million years. But at the same time, the author also highlights how much we do not know about the details of these processes, which we may never be able to figure out in detail. The reason for this is that the evidence for paleoanthropology, as for any historical science, is always fragmented and scarce. Therefore, there will always be questions that we will not manage to answer. But as Ian Tattersall explains, there are many crucial questions about who we are and where we come from that we have already managed to answer in sufficient detail. We are a unique hominin species that has dominated our planet, perhaps outcompeting any other with which our ancestors coexisted. But this only shows that we are an integral part of this natural world, which we need to respect and treat with modesty – we are not special in any nonbiological sense. The author invites you on a magnificent journey into the human past. Join him, and by the end of the book you will feel extremely rewarded, as you will have understood what it means to be human – biologically speaking.

Kostas Kampourakis, Series Editor

Preface

Homo sapiens is a strange animal. Not only do the requirements of our ungainly, two-footed posture reverberate in odd ways throughout our bodily anatomy, from our large, globular heads, balanced precariously atop our strangely curving vertical spines, right down to our springy, short-toed feet, but even more importantly, we human beings process information about ourselves and the world we inhabit in an unorthodox and entirely unprecedented way. Looking at this rather implausible creature, the proverbial Martian could be forgiven for concluding that human beings must have taken a very long time indeed to become so unlike other animals, including even our own closest living relatives, the great apes. Amazingly, though, our rather impressive fossil and archaeological records are telling us pretty clearly that the transition from a relatively run-of-the-mill large anthropoid to the world's most peculiar primate (outdoing even the bizarre aye-aye of Madagascar) happened amazingly fast, indeed in an evolutionary eyeblink: No animal alive in the world today is more radically unlike its own ancestor of a mere two million years ago than we *Homo sapiens* are.

This book is an attempt to explain that fast and bumpy human journey: a roller-coaster ride that currently appears to have begun somewhere in Africa, around seven million years ago, and that ultimately resulted in the colonization by *Homo sapiens* of every habitable corner of our planet. I say "appears," by the way, because understanding what happened during this epic odyssey is the province of paleoanthropology, a branch of science, and all scientific knowledge is by its nature provisional. Scientists are not trying to dispense wisdom for the ages. What they do endeavor to provide is the most accurate possible description of the observable world, and of the interactions that animate it, based on what they know at the time. The idea that scientists are out there searching for enduring "proof" of anything is one of humankind's supreme misconceptions, no matter how hard advertisers may try to convince you that the benefits of their products are "scientifically proven." Science progresses not by proving anything to be true forever, but by testing ideas about how the world works and systematically rejecting those that are shown to be false, thereby iterating toward an increasingly accurate picture of ourselves and our surroundings. It is this constant questioning and testing that most clearly distinguishes science from all the other ways humans have of knowing, and which explains why scientists are always hungry for new data – in the case of paleoanthropology, principally in the form of new fossils and of new information that sheds light on them.

This short book is thus necessarily a progress report, although by now so much is known of the human fossil past that it is very unlikely that a single future fossil discovery will send textbook writers scurrying to write new editions; and I have tried to paint with a sufficiently broad brush that much of the story it tells should prove reasonably durable. I will start by looking in Chapter 1 at evolution, the process that underwrites our human biological history, and without which we would not be here writing or reading about it. Evolution is itself a prime example of how ideas change. Charles Darwin's basic mid-nineteenth-century insight of descent with modification has been amazingly robust, but within my academic lifetime it has become widely understood (albeit perhaps less in paleoanthropology than in most evolutionary sciences) that the old equation of time with inexorable change needs to be abandoned. Readers wanting more detail on this would do well to consult Kostas Kampourakis's volume in this series, *Understanding Evolution*. In Chapter 2 I briefly examine some of the new technologies that are deepening and enlivening the study of the human past by allowing us to do such things as accurately dating fossils recovered from an amazing range of geological contexts; to peer at ancient diets; to "virtually" reconstruct badly distorted fossils; and to use variations in our genomes to understand the complex process by which modern humans took over the world.

In tackling the fossil evidence for human evolution, I first devote Chapters 3 and 4 to outlining the history of discovery in paleoanthropology. I do this separately from my review of the fossils themselves, because it is my firm belief that if we were to discover the entire human fossil afresh tomorrow, our interpretation of it would look very different from the one we currently espouse. Both the order in which fossils were found, and the preconceptions of their discoverers, have deeply affected not only the interpretations offered at the time, but also what we still believe today; and we are only able to understand why we hold our current beliefs about human evolution if we are consciously aware of what our predecessors believed before us. Separating history from discussion of the evidence in this way means that readers may find themselves paging back and forth a bit to find illustrations, for which I apologize; but I believe this disadvantage is amply compensated by the clarity imparted by introducing the characters before embarking on the play. For the reader's convenience, each chapter concludes with a table summarizing the principal extinct relatives discussed, and all hominin fossil sites (and some archaeological ones) that appear both in these chapters and elsewhere in the book are localized in the Maps section that precedes the text.

I then look at how we (or perhaps I should say I) interpret the human fossil record right now, bearing in mind that any account must basically be provisional. I do this chronologically, starting in Chapter 5 with the very early bipeds that ushered in the human story, before proceeding in Chapter 6 to the muddle around the emergence of our own genus *Homo*. In Chapter 7 I consider both *Homo heidelbergensis*, the first cosmopolitan hominin, and *H. neanderthalensis*, our best-known extinct relative; and in Chapter 8 I examine the emergence of our own species *Homo sapiens*, both as a physical entity and as a cognitive one, and glance at how our immediate predecessors so rapidly took over the world. It might be useful to note that graphics mapping how ancient populations moved may be found in a companion volume to this one, *Understanding Race*. Finally, in keeping with the convention established for this series, I conclude with a brief review of some major misunderstandings associated with the evolution of humankind.

Acknowledgments

Anyone writing about human evolution owes a huge practical and intellectual debt to every one of the innumerable scientists, living and departed, who helped to shape paleoanthropology as we currently understand it. May their contributions never be forgotten, especially in a world that seems ever more ready to dismiss the past as an irrelevance. On a more personal level I am deeply grateful to all the many colleagues, from all over the world, whose company, ideas, and often hospitality I have enjoyed over the past five decades. They are too numerous to mention individually here, but I extend my warmest thanks to all of them. I cannot, though, neglect to record my special gratitude to my amazing teachers, David Pilbeam and the late Elwyn Simons, as well as to four friends and colleagues with whom I have worked particularly closely over the years: Niles Eldredge, the late Bob Sussman, Jeffrey Schwartz, and Rob DeSalle. My associations with these extraordinary scientists taught me a great deal, hugely enlarged my perspective, and most importantly were a lot of fun. Parts of a draft of this book were kindly read and improved by Rob DeSalle, John Van Couvering, Will Harcourt-Smith, and David Hurst Thomas, none of whom is to blame for any of its remaining deficiencies.

One of the great pleasures of working in a very visual science is the opportunity it gives one to collaborate closely with some very gifted artists. I have been particularly fortunate in this regard, and the work of several of these colleagues is represented in this book. So my deepest thanks go, yet again, to Patricia Wynne, Jay Matternes, the late Nick Amorosi, Don McGranaghan, Diana Salles, Jennifer Steffey, and Kayla Younkin, whose enormous talents have not only given essential context to the written content of this book, but have made it so much more attractive to peruse.

I am also hugely indebted to Kostas Kampourakis, editor of Cambridge University Press's unique *Understanding Life* series, both for inviting me to write this volume and for suggesting numerous improvements to an initial draft. And at Cambridge University Press itself, I am immensely grateful to my editors, Katrina Halliday, who started the ball rolling, and Jessica Papworth, who steered the project to completion. Olivia Boult kept everything on track during the editorial process, and Sam Fearnley and Jenny van der Meijden cheerfully and efficiently saw the book through production in Cambridge, while Mathivathini Mareesan did the same in Pondicherry. Gary Smith undertook a very thoughtful copy-edit, and Judith Reading compiled the excellent index. My thanks to you all; working with everyone has been wonderfully rewarding.

1 Evolution

The Arrival of Evolutionary Thought

The notion that our planet and its inhabitants have not remained exactly as the Creator was supposed to have made them was in the air long before 1859, when the English natural historian Charles Darwin collected and published his evolutionary ideas in his great work *On the Origin of Species by Means of Natural Selection*. By that time, geologists had long known that the 6,000 years allowed by the Bible since the Creation was vastly inadequate for the sculpting of the current landscape by any natural mechanism; and the biologists who were just beginning to study the history of life via the fossil record were not far behind them. Around the turn of the nineteenth century, the French zoologist Jean-Baptiste Lamarck began to argue that fossil molluscan lineages from the Paris Basin had undergone structural change over time, and that the species concerned were consequently not fixed. Importantly, he implicated adaptation to the environment as the cause of change, although the means he suggested – subsequently infamous as "the inheritance of acquired characteristics" – brought later opprobrium. Soon afterwards, the Italian paleontologist Giambattista Brocchi, also working on marine invertebrates, observed that distinct species tended to replace one another abruptly in the sedimentary record of Tuscany. That led him to the idea that species, just like individuals, had births, histories, and deaths (by extinction). Births occurred when one species gave rise to another, so that lineages of organisms could actually diverge (and thereby eventually form branching trees).

The basic elements for recognizing and understanding evolution as a process of biotic change over time were thus in place almost half a century before Darwin wrote. What was added by Darwin – who devoured Lamarck's work, but may or may not have been exposed to Brocchi's ideas – was nonetheless revolutionary. In his masterwork, Darwin articulated and exhaustively documented his insight that the nested pattern of resemblances we see among organisms in nature is best explained by common ancestry. Physically similar organisms resemble one another not because the Creator wanted them that way, but because they share recent common ancestors. In turn, less similar organisms share remoter ancestry, degrees of difference being due to the accumulation of physical changes in ancestor–descendant lineages as a function of time. Darwin framed his argument for common descent with astonishing erudition and finesse, forcefully bringing his radical ideas to the attention of a largely orthodox Christian scientific community and public that was, at last, prepared to be at least partially receptive. Not that the enterprise would be easy. Darwin delayed publishing his evolutionary thoughts for many years out of a fear of public (and his devout wife's) reaction; and he was particularly at pains not to draw attention to the pretty obvious implication that, as an animal and a primate, *Homo sapiens* necessarily has an evolutionary history too. Indeed, all he said on that subject in the *Origin* was that "light will be shed on the history of man and his origins." Still, although Darwin had correctly foreseen the uproar that would break out when his book was published, the clamor subsided more quickly than he might have anticipated. By the end of the nineteenth century a secularizing British public had largely come to terms with its (broadly) ape ancestry, leaving the scientists to squabble over details of process.

Darwin's own thumbnail characterization of his theory of evolution was "descent with modification." This is a wonderfully succinct summary of the process that gave us the stunning structural diversity we see among living forms today, via the accumulation of heritable changes in a long series of lineages that successively forked out from a single common ancestor. That ancestor probably lived as much as four billion years ago, and its tens of millions of living descendants are as different as bacteria, bushes, and bobcats. Darwin's explanation of how this could have happened – a major selling point in his time, though vigorously debated subsequently – involved what he termed "natural selection": a concept that was so intuitively reasonable as to have (as legend has it) caused his close colleague Thomas Huxley to slap his forehead and exclaim, "How stupid not to have thought of that!"

Darwin knew that all living species are variable, and he came to believe that fact to be critically important. What is more, although he had no idea (or, more correctly, an erroneous one) of how biological inheritance works (he accepted the inheritance of acquired characters), he was very conscious of the fact that most physical features are parentally inherited. Darwin also knew that breeders, by carefully selecting which individuals in a population will reproduce, are able to induce very rapid and substantial changes in lineages of domestic animals and plants. So, why not Mother Nature? Darwin reasoned that in any variable population some individuals are inevitably better endowed than others in hereditary traits that enhance their survival and reproduction; and because those better adapted ("fitter") individuals will survive and reproduce more successfully than the rest, their descendants and their favorable traits will inevitably multiply in the population with the passage of time and the generations, even as inferior adaptations disappear. Repeated over enough generations, this blind natural process of selection of fitter individuals will slowly and inevitably transform each species/lineage, with only time and circumstance limiting the amount of accumulated change possible. Darwin also knew, of course, that lineage splitting, and not just change within each lineage, had to be important in generating the amazing diversity that we see in the living and fossil worlds.

Genetics and the Modern Evolutionary Synthesis

Darwin's concept of evolutionary change by natural selection depended on the passing down, from parent to offspring, of inherited characteristics; but it had been formulated in the absence of an accurate notion of how heredity worked. That gap began to be filled at the turn of the twentieth century. Back in the 1860s, the Augustinian friar Gregor Mendel had studied heredity in flowering peas he grew in his monastery garden; and although he published his results in a local journal that was read by few (Darwin is rumored not even to have cut the pages in his copy), he is generally given credit for the principles of "Mendelian" inheritance that were separately worked out in three different European biology laboratories in 1900, following the confirmation in 1883 that the hereditary information was carried in the mother's ovum and the father's sperm. Those principles, which launched the modern science of genetics, included the notion that hereditary features are independently passed along under the control of discrete, paired (one from each parent) hereditary units. Those units do not blend in the offspring, but are passed instead from one generation to the next intact and undiluted. A "recessive" element from one parent will not be expressed in the offspring's "phenotype" (physical appearance) if a "dominant" form is received from the other; but it is always there nonetheless, ready to be passed along in turn. It was not long before those hereditary units had been dubbed "genes" (their alternative forms were called "alleles"), and the term "mutation" had been applied to the spontaneous changes in the genes that provide the variation on which evolution acts.

Various other observations were quickly made. For one thing, rather than being dichotomous, most characteristics vary continuously in their expression in populations (think of physical strength or visual acuity, for example). That is because the development of most characters is controlled not by single genes, but by many of them working together. It was also quickly determined that the environment played an important role in the determination of phenotypes, and in addition most genes turned out to play a role in the determination of many different physical characteristics. Putting all this together gave birth to the science of population genetics, which mathematically models the behaviors of genes in populations; and in 1918 the English quantitative geneticist R. A. Fisher published his "infinitesimal model" that sees most phenotypes as the result of a very complex interplay between numerous genes, on the one hand, and the environment, on the other. At around this time it was also realized that, especially in small populations, random factors (known as "drift") could also play a significant role in the fate of newly appearing variants.

During the first quarter of the twentieth century, biologists vigorously debated the relationship of genetic processes to evolutionary change. It was soon recognized that those spontaneous mutations were copying errors that constantly occurred in the genes as they were duplicated in the production of new cells, including the reproductive ones. Most such errors resulted in weakened function, and hence their bearers could be weeded out by selection. Others might be neutral with respect to function, and thus might either quietly disappear, or simply hang around, as a matter of chance. But functionally valuable new alleles can provide the new variation on which evolutionary change thrives; and indeed, "mutation pressure" consequently became a favorite driver of evolution, the speed at which genes mutated controlling the rapidity with which evolutionary change could take place. As such considerations were introduced, natural selection became only one of several contenders for agency in evolutionary change. But things shook out quite rapidly, so that by the end of the 1920s Fisher and other mathematical modelers had laid the groundwork for the development of what would become known as the "Modern Evolutionary Synthesis." Following the lead of the Russian-born geneticist Theodosius Dobzhansky, working in the USA, geneticists, systematists (students of diversity in nature), and paleontologists came together in a tacit agreement that evolution was largely propelled by the long-term action of natural selection on lineages of organisms. Change came as the frequencies of old and new alleles in those populations shifted under selection, with the outcome of keeping them in equilibrium with changing environments, or improving their adaptation to stable ones. Evolution was all about gradual adaptation.

This "neo-Darwinian" perspective threw the emphasis back on to slow change within lineages. And it had the presumably unintended effect of making species recognition problematic in the dimension of time. Species had been recognized since the seventeenth century as the basic "natural" unit in the living world; and the ornithologist Ernst Mayr, in addition to being one of the giants of the Synthesis, was also a leading proponent of the "biological" view of species, seeing them as the largest unit in nature within which interbreeding among individuals may freely take place. In this view, the larger taxonomic units ("taxa"), such as the genera into which species are grouped, the families into which genera are grouped, and the orders into which families are assembled, are simply products of the human propensity to classify, while in contrast the limits of species are determined by the reproductive choices or performances of their own members. There are now some 30 different definitions of the species on offer, partly because it turns out that members of very closely related but nonetheless differentiated species may indulge in reproductive activities if given a chance; but the biological definition would still probably be the choice of most working vertebrate systematists – if they were forced to choose.

Mayr was also a leader in working out the biogeographical implications of the fact that species evolve from other species, and he especially espoused the notion that most vertebrate species can differentiate only when they are in isolation. In other words, a subpopulation can develop the genetic incompatibility with its parental population that will make it a different species only when genetic exchange between the two is interrupted. Such incompatibility might be expressed anatomically, behaviorally, or simply in impaired reproductive performance. Just for the record, early in his career Darwin had thought hard about this matter, too. However, while he recognized that various bird lineages in the Galapagos archipelago had differentiated in isolation on their respective islands, he ran into difficulty visualizing how isolation could have been achieved on the continents. Mayr had no such problem, because by his day it was already well established that instability in past climates and environments, plus what we now call tectonic events, had repeatedly interrupted the continuity of habitats worldwide. But Mayr's paleontological colleagues had to face the awkward reality that, in the dimension of time that was their bailiwick, the Synthesis saw species not as discrete units with reproductive boundaries, however blurry, but as steadily modifying lineages in which earlier stages inevitably evolved themselves out of existence as the years passed.

That made life difficult for the paleontologists, whose job it was to make sense of the fossil record. That was because, if they were both to describe an ancient world comparable to today's, and to adhere to the principles of the Synthesis, paleontologists had not only to diagnose distinct species in the fossil record, but also to recognize that those species were inherently undiagnosable, since there were in principle no boundaries between them. Any division of a gradually evolving continuum was necessarily arbitrary, so that not only was the attempt to do so intellectually unsatisfying, but whatever you chose to do would, even in principle, be subject to endless inconclusive argument. In its early and more nuanced versions the Synthesis was open to recognizing complexities such as this. But – almost inevitably, given the human love of reductionist explanation – it gradually "hardened" to become a dogma, at the center of which lay the slow, gradual modification of lineages by natural selection. Species as "real," bounded, entities took a back seat; and even the paleontologists went along with this as, under the reductive and seductive sway of the Synthesis, they ignored the skimpy nature of the emperor's clothing. And, as we see in Chapter 3, it was in its hardened form that the Synthesis was eventually introduced into paleoanthropology, by none other than Ernst Mayr himself.

Punctuated Equilibria

Given the fact that the Synthesis had relegated paleontologists to the essentially clerical task of clearing up the details of Life's history, leaving to others the more interesting pursuit of discovering its great patterns, it is hardly surprising that the first rumblings of discontent came from students of the fossil record. Long before the Synthesis intruded, Darwin's paleontologist colleague Hugh Falconer had already been impressed by how long distinctive mammal and other species lingered in the rocks of the Siwalik Hills in India, over a total period now known to be around four million years (myr). But so heavy lay the hand of the Synthesis that such observations were ignored, and it was not until 1971 that Niles Eldredge, a paleontologist at New York City's American Museum of Natural History (where Ernst Mayr had spent his early career) upset the applecart. In that year Eldredge published a summary of the conclusions he'd reached in his doctoral thesis on Devonian trilobites (bottom-dwelling marine invertebrates) from the US Midwest and upper New York State. And rather than try to fit his fossil data into the rigid structure of the reigning Synthesis, Eldredge allowed himself to discover a very different evolutionary pattern: one that was similar, as he would later find out, to the one Giambattista Brocchi had discerned in Tuscany a century and a half earlier. The picture he saw was overwhelmingly one of stability (stasis): Over a 6-myr span in the Midwest, there was only a single significant event in his group of interest, the abrupt replacement of a particular trilobite species by a close relative. Eldredge saw basically the same thing at sites in New York; but at one quarry there he found both kinds of trilobite together, and concluded that he had stumbled on a place where an event of speciation had actually been in progress roughly 400 myr ago. The most parsimonious scenario was that, for an extended period, the parental trilobite species had been ubiquitous in the Devonian shallow seas that covered much of what was to become the United States; that a rapid speciation event had occurred close to the eastern periphery of its distribution; and that the descendant species had then spread out to replace its progenitor throughout its range. Not at all what the Synthesis would have predicted!

Eldredge then joined forces with his colleague Stephen Jay Gould to generalize this finding, and at a meeting the next year they jointly presented the notion of "Punctuated Equilibria" to replace the "Phyletic Gradualism" of the Synthesis. Evolution, they claimed, rather than being a gradual affair, was more commonly episodic in nature. It largely involved the interruption of longer or shorter periods of stasis by short-term speciation events associated with morphological innovation; and the changes visible in the fossil record were often driven by abrupt climatic and environmental shifts that made perfection of adaptation irrelevant. All of which meant, of course, that many of the famous "breaks" in the fossil record (i.e., the lack of expected intermediates) might encode real information about evolutionary histories, rather than simply reflecting deficiencies of preservation. It also returned species to the status of "real" entities, bounded in time as well as in space. As Brocchi's early-nineteenth-century observations had suggested, species indeed had origins at speciation; finite but often long lifespans during which descendant species might bud off as peripheral populations were isolated and went their own ways; and, eventually, deaths when extinction came. Once more, paleontologists were at liberty to study objective, bounded entities.

This questioning of a comfortable received wisdom provoked a widespread initial outcry and such mirthful characterizations as "evolution by jerks." But soon evolutionary biologists came to terms with punctuated equilibria as a phenomenon to be dealt with, even though many continued to believe that gradual natural selection still had an important place in evolutionary change. In my case, these findings caused me to reconsider everything I had been taught. I realized that thinking in terms of natural selection had taken the focus away from the species itself, transferring it to characteristics of the individual. And yet, what ultimate good is it to be the most excellently adapted example of your species, in whatever feature, if your entire species is being outcompeted into extinction? Or if your survival or reproductive success will be largely a matter of chance, as they very often are? Still, the force of tradition is strong, and paleoanthropologists continue to speak blithely of the "evolution of the foot," or the "evolution of the brain," or the "evolution of the gut," without properly digesting the fact that all these structures are inextricably embedded in whole functioning organisms, and that it is those organisms, not their individual features, that are triaged by nature. In the real world you succeed or fail as a complete being, not as a foot, or a brain, or a digestive system. What is more, each gene has many jobs to do, so that changing any one feature may lead to undesirable alterations in others.

The bottom line is, then, that selection can only fine-tune a particular feature within a species if that feature happens to be absolutely critical for individual survival or reproductive success. It is almost certainly no accident, for example, that the male chimpanzees who must compete constantly for access to females have huge testicles (almost as big as their brains), while the silverback gorilla males that almost effortlessly dominate their harems do not. And success in competition among related taxa may hinge on tiny differences: The astonishingly rapid replacement in the United States of earlier variants of the SARS-CoV-2 virus by the new variant (Lineage B.1.1.7) first identified in the UK seems to have been due to increased transmissibility attributable to a minor modification to its spike protein.

Of course, nature is a very complex place; and it is always possible to find a striking exception to almost any generalization you might care to make about it. Nonetheless, it does seem reasonably fair to say that, especially among intensely social organisms such as the primates, it is often sufficient to be good enough just to get by. The excellence of your individual adaptation(s) may not be of great relevance in a world where social cushioning exists, and where so much also depends on chance. Your expertise as a climber, for example, will hardly help much in a drying environment in which trees are disappearing. Indeed, it occurred to me very early that, while natural selection is a mathematical certainty in a world in which more individuals are born than survive to reproduce (while I was writing this a robin's nest outside my window, containing four voracious chicks, was rudely raided by a crow that randomly murdered them all), its main function is to trim off the extremes of the spectrum of variability within each species, thereby maintaining the "fitness" of the species itself to survive and reproduce, rather than that of the individuals composing it. To caricature for the sake of effect, if as a biped you are born with one leg or three, you are less likely to survive and reproduce successfully than you are if you have the standard two. This function is known as "stabilizing selection," and it is of critical value in keeping entire lineages viable in the face of the genomic tendency to mutate.

Finally, we need to bear in mind that external events occurring entirely randomly with respect to adaptation have probably been the most critical evolutionary drivers of all. It is, for example, almost certainly no accident that our own genus *Homo* evolved, and very rapidly modified, during the Pleistocene ("Ice Ages") epoch. This was a time when major climatic swings routinely occurred even within individual lifetimes. On the species level, such circumstances not only repeatedly created the conditions for speciation via successive population isolations, but also the conditions for competition when those populations were reunited when conditions swung back. And at a higher level, large excursions in climate and habitat were often associated with major biotic turnovers during which entire faunas were replaced. Specifically in the human case, which involved a cultural, large-brained, and particularly pragmatic creature, such changes may sometimes have favored behavioral rather than physical accommodation – which, as we will see, may have had a lot to do with the remarkable speed with which humans evolved over the last two million years.

A Revolution in Systematics

Right around the time when the notion of punctuated equilibria was beginning to force a rethinking of evolutionary process, an analogous revolution was taking place in systematics, the science that deals with the diversity and classification of organisms. Until the middle of the twentieth century, the business of recognizing and classifying units in nature had largely been a matter of expert opinion. Knowledgeable people declared what they thought; and that was that. It was very tough to challenge the opinion of an acknowledged expert because it was his (very occasionally her) word against yours; and, if he or she was famous, you were usually out of luck. But in 1950 a German entomologist called Willi Hennig challenged all this by proposing a testable approach to systematics, one that unfortunately did not have much international impact until his book was translated into English 16 years later as *Phylogenetic Systematics*. But once the cry had been taken up by the American Museum of Natural History systematists Donn Rosen and Gary Nelson, Hennig's approach (dubbed "cladistics" by Ernst Mayr) rapidly overturned the practice of systematics everywhere, naturally enough after much vociferous complaining.

The core of Hennig's system lay in the recognition of "monophyletic" groups (of organisms all descended from the same common ancestor) on the basis of homology: of possessing derived ("apomorphic") characters inherited from that ancestor. General resemblance was not enough: Independently evolved similarities or "convergences" (such as wings in insects, birds, and bats) were irrelevant to common ancestry. And once a character had been used to unite a group (for example, four legs in the tetrapod group that includes all terrestrial vertebrates), it was no longer of systematic utility; all relationships within the tetrapod group had to be established based on other features (e.g., milk production in mammals, feathers in birds). The geometry of ancestry and descent within any group of living or fossil taxa was summarized in a branching diagram, known as a "cladogram," in which known taxa lay at the branch tips and the ancestor was always hypothetical, inferred from the characteristics of the descendant group to which it gave rise. A group of organisms descended from a particular common ancestor was called a "clade." What was important about cladograms, and what distinguished them from earlier kinds of family trees, was that they were testable. It was always potentially possible to falsify a cladogram by adding new characters or taxa to the analysis.

One observation that constructing cladograms for many groups rapidly brought to light was just how rampant homoplasy (convergence, or independent acquisition of similar characteristics) is in nature. And equally intriguingly, using this approach helped us to understand just how few known fossil forms conform to what we would expect for the hypothetical ancestor of the group to which they are assigned. That is because an ancestor is necessarily primitive (unchanged) in every character relative to every other member of its group, a condition that practical experience showed to be rarely, if ever, satisfied by an actual fossil. But then again, if a form is primitive in all respects, it will offer no derived characters to link it to its presumed descendants!

In the early days, what was primitive and what was derived was mainly inferred from the distribution of characters within the larger clade. Commonly occurring characters were more likely primitive, whereas those found in only one taxon, or just a few, were more probably derived. And if you could also find a particular character (or, more properly, character *state*) in a close relative outside the group under immediate consideration, it was plausibly primitive and thus not usable for linking subgroups within the taxon of interest. At first, cladograms were put together by hand (or, rather, by mind), which naturally limited the number of characters that could be employed in a particular analysis. But soon computer-based quantitative methods that could handle large numbers of characters were introduced, and they are overwhelmingly the choice among systematists today. These methods use various approaches to digest large data sets, the two leaders being parsimony and likelihood. When parsimony is used, numerous possible trees are generated for the group being analyzed, each of their dichotomously forking branches bearing at its tip one of that group's component taxa (usually a species or a genus). Each candidate tree is then evaluated for the number of changes in character states needed to construct it, and the tree requiring the lowest number of changes (hence parsimony) is the one preferred. Some biologists, arguing that nature is not necessarily always parsimonious, prefer to estimate the relative probabilities ("likelihoods") of all possible tree geometries, given something already known about the group of interest. These two approaches are ubiquitous nowadays in systematic biology, and they have been tried in paleoanthropology. However, within a group as close-knit as the one containing human beings it is difficult to create extensive and reliable matrices of distinct character states for the computers to get their teeth into, so neither approach has become a routine part of the paleoanthropological armamentarium – except where DNA is involved. Largely, this is because DNA data sets are mind-bogglingly enormous, well suited to quantitative analysis, and impossible to understand in any other way. But it must also be admitted that, for the historical reasons we will encounter in Chapters 3 and 4, paleoanthropologists have rarely thought systematics itself to be very important.

A Very Brief History of Life

Human beings are extreme latecomers to Earth and its biota. The history of life on Earth goes back to remarkably soon after the planet condensed, about 4.5 billion years ago, from a cloud of gas and dust that swirled about the early Sun. By about 3.7 billion years ago, microorganisms were already leaving chemical signatures in the most ancient rocks preserved in Earth's hardening surface, and by about 3.5 billion years ago stromatolites – layered microbial mats – were becoming a feature in the fossil record. At this time, the planet's atmosphere consisted mainly of carbon dioxide, with lots of water vapor and some methane and ammonia; but that rapidly changed with the advent some 2.4 billion years ago of the cyanobacteria, single-celled photosynthetic organisms that produced oxygen as a metabolic by-product. The seas in which the cyanobacteria lived abounded in iron molecules, and most of the oxygen they produced initially became bound to that iron, sinking to the sea floor and forming deep series of banded iron deposits that have subsequently provided a bonanza to modern mining companies. Once the free iron was all bound, the oxygen produced by the cyanobacteria began to accumulate in the atmosphere. This allowed the evolution of the "eukaryotic" cell that, unlike the simple bacterial cell in which the DNA floats free, keeps its DNA confined inside a membrane-bound nucleus and houses several specialized "organelles" within its outer membrane.

Groups of such cells soon began to cohabit, leading ultimately to the emergence of the first animals at around 800 myr ago. Those early animals were probably sessile, siphoning nutrients from the sea around them; but more complex sponge-like forms soon followed, and during the Ediacaran period, around 600 myr ago, animals began to diversify vigorously. By the end of the Ediacaran, atmospheric and dissolved oxygen had increased sufficiently to sustain oxygen-dependent organisms, and in the following Devonian period (see Figure 1.1 for the succession of geological time units) there was an "explosion" of animal forms in the oceans. This Devonian diversification involved the emergence of most of the major animal groups (phyla) that are familiar today, including the Vertebrata (backboned animals), to which we belong.

The late Devonian saw the origin of the tetrapods, the vertebrate group that first left the ocean to colonize the continents. Descended from "lobe-finned" fishes that had skeletal structures within their pelvic and pectoral fins, terrestrial vertebrates are first known from fossils in the 385-myr range, although some 397-myr-old trackways from Poland are believed to have been made by

Eon	Era	System/ Period	Age Myr
	Cenozoic	Quaternary	0.0118
		Neogene	1.8
		Paleogene	23.0
			65.5
	Mesozoic	Cretaceous	
		Jurassic	145.5
		Triassic	199.6
Phanerozoic			251.0
	Paleozoic	Permian	
		Carboniferous	299.0
		Devonian	359.2
		Silurian	416.0
		Ordovician	443.7
		Cambrian	488.3
			542.0
Precambrian — Proterozoic	Neo-Proterozoic	Ediacaran	630
		Cryogenian	850
		Tonian	1000
	Meso-Proterozoic	Stenian	1200
		Ectasian	1400
		Calymmian	1600
	Paleo-Proterozoic	Statherian	1800
		Orosirian	2050
		Rhyacian	2300
		Siderian	2500
Precambrian — Archean		Neoarchean	2800
		Mesoarchean	3200
		Paleoarchean	3600
		Eoarchean	

Cenozoic detail

Era	System/ Period	Series/ Epoch	Age Myr
Cenozoic	Quaternary	Holocene	0.0118
		Pleistocene	
			1.8
	Neogene	Pliocene	
			5.3
		Miocene	
			23.0
	Paleogene	Oligocene	
			33.9
		Eocene	
			55.8
		Paleocene	
			65.5

Figure 1.1 Simplified International Stratigraphic Chart showing the major divisions of Earth history, with current datings. On the right, a Cenozoic time chart with greater detail.

tetrapods. The following Carboniferous period saw the ancestors of today's amphibians and reptiles emerge. Flowering plants were yet to evolve, but ferns and primitive conifers dominated the landscape, notably forming wetland forests that produced extensive coal deposits and were ravaged by fires fueled by skyrocketing levels of atmospheric oxygen. That extra oxygen also allowed enormous insects to evolve (think dragonflies with a three-foot wingspan).

The following Permian period witnessed the arrival of the "mammal-like reptiles," a lumbering group somewhere within which the origin of today's mammals may ultimately lie. At the end of both the Devonian and the Permian periods, large "mass extinctions" occurred in which a large proportion of all the species living on the planet disappeared, leading each time to the rapid diversification of a new fauna. One usually hears of five major mass extinction events in the ancient past (usually ascribed to natural catastrophes of one kind or another); but it should be kept in mind that mass extinction is a relatively common phenomenon, even if it rarely happens on quite the scale of the "big five."

The Triassic period that followed the end-Permian extinction witnessed the origin and diversification of the dinosaurs, as well as the appearance of the first recognizable mammals; and in the subsequent Jurassic period birds first showed up, as an offshoot of the theropod dinosaurs. During the Cretaceous period, the last of the Mesozoic Era, mammals quietly diversified even as dinosaurs dominated the terrestrial landscape. Some authorities believe that the roots of at least some of the living mammalian orders must lie in the Cretaceous, but there is currently little fossil evidence for this although the great modern placental and marsupial mammal groups clearly had their origins in this period. At the end of the Cretaceous, some 66 myr ago (when the diversity of dinosaurs may already have been waning, though this is disputed), a huge bolide impact caused an environmental cataclysm that carried away not just the dinosaurs but 60 percent of the entire biota, leaving the terrestrial field open to the small-bodied and principally nocturnal mammals.

Those surviving mammals promptly diversified, and by the end of the Eocene epoch some 34 myr ago the terrestrial fauna had taken on a fairly modern look, with mammal orders as disparate as bats, primates, anteaters, ungulates, and shrews dominating terrestrial ecosystems, while whales and seals multiplied in the seas. The primates of the period are most closely matched by today's lemurs, which are relatively small-brained and still highly dependent on the sense of smell. Primates of the anthropoid group to which we belong did not emerge significantly until the short next epoch, the Oligocene; but in the following Miocene epoch, beginning at around 23 myr ago, the modern South American and Old-World monkey families became well established, along with the ape superfamily to which humans belong. Early apes flourished and vigorously diversified in the Miocene forests of Africa and Eurasia, but later in the epoch, as climates began to dry out and become more seasonal and the forests correspondingly changed in nature and shrank, their numbers dwindled. Today, this formerly very diverse group is represented only by orangutans in Sulawesi and Borneo; by chimpanzees, bonobos, and gorillas in equatorial Africa; and by its most thoroughly errant member, *Homo sapiens*, everywhere.

The earliest members of our subfamily Homininae (formerly known as the family Hominidae; the difference is notional for our purposes, though the group is certainly diverse enough to deserve full family status) emerged toward the end of the Miocene, some 7 myr ago. The subfamily diversified quite energetically during the short Pliocene epoch that began at about 5.3 myr ago following an amazing environmental event known as the "Messinian salinity crisis." During this episode, the Mediterranean Sea was isolated from the Atlantic due to compression at Gibraltar from a northward-moving African continent, and it almost entirely dried up. The Pliocene yielded to the Pleistocene ("Ice Ages") epoch at a date that has recently been arbitrarily changed (to the chagrin of many) to about 2.6 myr ago, a point that lies close to both a major geomagnetic reversal (evidence for which can be found in rocks worldwide – see the next chapter) and the onset of a climatic cooling phase. It does not, however, coincide with any realistic concept of the origin of our genus *Homo* – which is nonetheless often, if inaccurately, said to have appeared at around that time. Recognizable early *Homo* (in the sense of creatures bearing significant similarity and relationship to modern humans) came into existence at around 2 myr ago, during a period of further climatic deterioration.

About 1 myr ago the world climate settled into cycling every 100,000 years (100 kyr) or so between warmer intervals ("interglacials") that were broadly comparable to the present, and troughs of intense cold ("glacials"). Many smaller oscillations occurred in between, sometimes on extremely short time-scales. During this time, ice sheets expanded and contracted across the northern continents, with colder times at higher latitudes translating broadly into arid periods in the tropics. The last glacial ended at about 12 kyr ago, giving way to the Holocene epoch in which we are now. We are often said to be currently in the "Anthropocene," but this age thankfully has no formal status, and it has in any event been much too short so far to amount to anything more than a stratigraphic anomaly. It certainly doesn't yet warrant formal recognition as an epoch. As we will see, over the course of the Pleistocene epoch various species of *Homo* came and went until, at around 200 kyr ago, our own species *Homo sapiens* originated in Africa and quickly took over the world.

2 Technology: Dating, Diets, and Development

The Impact of Technology on Our Understanding of Human Evolution

Within the lifetimes of some of today's older paleontologists, the armamentarium available to those who studied fossils was pretty limited, consisting mainly of hands, brain, and a rock hammer. A fossil, by the way, is any evidence of past life: An ancient footprint or worm burrow is technically a fossil, although as far as mammals like us are concerned the vast majority of fossils are the mineralized remains of bones and teeth. These are the hardest tissues of the body, and thus have the best chance of being preserved in the rock record. For reference, Figure 2.1 shows a human skeleton with the major bones identified.

What a paleontologist traditionally did was to go out into the field and collect fossils from sediments that could probably be fitted reasonably well into the long sequence of events at the Earth's surface – but that, frustratingly, couldn't be assigned a year date. Once back in the laboratory those fossils probably needed to be painstakingly freed, by hand, from their rocky matrices. Then they could be identified and classified, and even reconstructed if there was enough material. From the ensemble of fossils found in a locality, and maybe from sedimentary evidence, specialists could glean an impression of the environment in which their original owners had lived; and from their physical structures they could make an educated guess about how their subjects had functioned in life. And then they would be ready to form their expert opinions.

All of that has changed dramatically in the last three-quarters of a century. Now it is possible to assign accurate year-dates to fossils recovered from

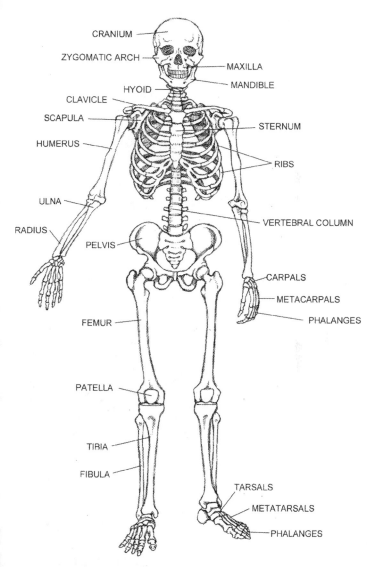

Figure 2.1 A modern human skeleton, with the major bones identified.

a remarkable range of burial contexts. Reconstructions can be done "virtually" on computer screens, without the need to carve delicate bone away from its rocky encasement. Geochemical and powerful microscopic techniques reveal intimate details of ancient diets. Computer modeling can help reveal ancient gaits, and tiny growth rings in the teeth, visible only at unimaginable magnifications, will even tell you at what age an individual was weaned. The DNA that is sometimes retrievable from relatively recent fossils will inform you about population structure and relationships in bygone species. And on and on. Paleoanthropology is now truly an interdisciplinary science, involving specialists from an ever-widening array of fields. In the chapters to come we will return to all these disciplines, and others; the short account in the present chapter can only scratch the surface of what is now possible, looking briefly at a sample of the most important technologies that are now available to enlighten us about the lives of our long-vanished ancestors.

How Old Is It?

Fossils usually take the form of mineralized bones and teeth of long-dead animals, although they can technically be any direct evidence of ancient life: plant impressions, footprints, and so on. And, naturally enough, the first thing anyone wants to know about a fossil is, "how old is it?" That sounds like a simple question, but it was not one that could be answered with a number before the middle of the twentieth century. Before that point, only "relative" dating had been available: older than this, younger than that. Geologists placed sedimentary rock layers (and any fossils they contained) within a visible local geological sequence that could, hopefully, be correlated with other sequences nearby. But because physical correlation of rock sequences over long distances was often difficult or impossible, it was the fossil species themselves, with their limited lifespans, that were often used as indicators of age, with closely related species in different parts of the world being assigned to the same general period of time. By the end of the nineteenth century, endless local repetition of such procedures had produced the succession of geological time units we still use today. Geologists divided the long stretch of Earth's history since the (then) first-known fossils into three long eras (in order, the Paleozoic, the Mesozoic, and the Cenozoic), each one divided into several periods which were, in turn, subdivided into epochs (Figure 1.1). As we now know, the human family did not appear until right at the end of the Cenozoic era, in the late Miocene epoch.

Everything changed for paleoanthropology in 1946, with the invention of radiocarbon dating. That revolutionary method of "absolute" dating in years depended on the clock-like regularity with which unstable radioactive isotopes (alternative forms of an element) spontaneously "decay" to stable states of lower energy. The half-life of the unstable ^{14}C isotope of carbon (the time it takes for half of any quantity of it to decay) is a quick 5,730 years. While they are alive, organisms maintain their radioactive carbon in a constant ratio with the stable version; but after they die the decay clock starts ticking, as the quantity of ^{14}C in the remains starts to diminish at a constant rate. So, if you compare the amount of radioactive to stable carbon in an organic sample (charcoal from a fire, say, or a turtle scute, or even a fossil bone if there is enough organic material left in it), and apply the half-life, you can derive a pretty good estimate of time elapsed since death. In practice things get a bit more complicated, because the ambient amount of ^{14}C has varied over time; but precise modern methods of calibration and measurement can yield pretty reliable dates using very tiny samples. The drawback for paleoanthropologists is that the rather short half-life of ^{14}C and the loss of organics in samples limits the use of the method to the last 50 kyr or so, although this admittedly covers an interesting period in the human story.

Still, help was on the way for those interested in earlier periods. The year 1961 saw the first use in paleoanthropology of the potassium–argon dating method, in which researchers measure the accumulation of the stable gas argon in rock samples as the radioactive potassium isotope ^{40}K decays. The K/Ar clock starts running when hot rock becomes cold enough to begin trapping the argon daughter product, as occurs for example when volcanic rocks such as extruded lava flows or ashfalls start cooling on the landscape. That makes the technique particularly valuable when scientists want to date fossil-bearing sediments that are interspersed with lava flows and tuff-falls, such as is typically the case in the Plio-Pleistocene of East Africa's Rift Valley: The dates of fossils can then be interpolated from the ages of volcanic rocks bracketing the sediments that contain them. At about 1.2 billion years the half-life of radioactive potassium is extremely long, so the quantities of argon accumulated in very recently cooled rocks are not precisely measurable.

This means that, although a more accurate descendant technique known as argon–argon (^{39}Ar/^{40}Ar) dating has been used on rocks as young as 250 kyr or even younger, there is still a significant gap until radiocarbon dating can be used.

As it happens, most of the human fossils that fall in that gap have been recovered not from conventional stratigraphic contexts out on the landscape, but from accumulations in the caves in which humans seem increasingly to have sought shelter over the later Pleistocene. Several "trapped-charge" methods are among the techniques that have been used to date fossils in this period. One of them, known as thermoluminescence (TL), has been successfully used on samples between about 1,000 and 500,000 years old. The TL method measures the light emitted from a crystalline mineral sample when it is heated, the brightness of that light being a function of the number of trapped electrons released from defects in its crystal lattice. That number is proportional both to time and to the local background radiation, so that if the latter is known it is possible to calculate the time elapsed since the last time the sample was heated (and the lattice emptied) or exposed to sunlight. Optically stimulated luminescence dating (OSL) is a related method that releases those trapped electrons, most commonly in quartz grains, by using a light stimulus. In a similar vein, electron spin resonance (ESR) dating was used as early as the 1970s to date the formation of cave carbonate deposits. The accumulation of electrons trapped in lattice defects in the carbonate crystals is measured by the eponymous ESR spectrometry, in which specimens are placed in a magnetic field and bombarded with microwaves. The method has since been widely employed on the enamel of fossil teeth as young as 10 kyr, and as old as 3 myr.

Also widely used in limestone-cave contexts is uranium–thorium (U-series) dating, which has proven a particularly useful technique for dating cave calcites. Those calcites consist not only of the stalagmites and stalactites that make many limestone caves so beautiful, but also of the chemically identical sheets of flowstone that are deposited on their walls and floors by moving water. These can provide capping or minimum dates for deposits beneath or above them, and they may sometimes bracket archaeological or fossil-bearing layers. Soluble in water, radioactive uranium-234 is deposited in the flowstones as they are formed. It then begins to decay (with a half-life of 245 kyr) to insoluble thorium-230, of which none will originally have been present. That thorium is itself unstable, decaying with a half-life of about 75 kyr, but an age can nonetheless be calculated from the ratio of the two isotopes (relatively easily measured by mass spectrometry). The utility of this system extends back to around 350 kyr or perhaps a little more.

Cosmogenic nuclide dating, a relatively recent entrant, is one of a set of "surface exposure" dating methods that is coming into increasing use in paleoanthropology. The eponymous radioactive cosmogenic nuclides (most commonly beryllium-10 and aluminum-26) are products of bombardment of Earth's surface by cosmic rays. When an object originally on or near the surface is buried deeper than about a meter, production of the nuclides ceases and the "burial age" can subsequently be calculated from nuclide abundance measured using accelerator mass spectrometry. Accurate knowledge of production rates is key, and makes the use of two nuclides imperative. The production rate ratio of $^{26}Al/^{10}Be$ in quartz, the mineral to which the method is most often applied, decays with a half-life of 1.36 myr, making the method applicable in the range from around 10 kyr to 10 myr. In paleoanthropology, cosmogenic nuclides have been used to date the time elapsed since bones or artifacts were buried in sediments that were previously exposed to cosmic radiation.

From time to time Earth's magnetic field reverses. This has provided an independent way to seriate past events, because rocks retain a record of the direction of magnetization at the time they were laid down. Calibration using absolute dating has allowed the development of a "palaeomagnetic time-scale" that extends back to cover the events in hominin evolution. So, while compass needles have pointed north since about 780 kyr ago, before then they had done so only periodically, for instance between 0.9 and 1.06 myr ago, briefly at 1.19 myr ago, and between 1.78 and 2.0 myr ago. In the intervening years they would have pointed south. The paleomagnetic orientation of sediments at a particular hominin site cannot, of course, give you a date on its own; but in combination with other information it can place sediments within the established and independently dated paleomagnetic sequence.

Any list of the absolute and relative dating techniques now available could go on and on, though whether one method or another is appropriate or usable in a particular case depends on the nature and age of the site concerned. Still,

Method	Material Dated	Range	Half-Life
Radiocarbon (^{14}C)	5,730 yr	Organics	<50 kyr
Potassium–argon (and argon–argon)	1.2 byr	Volcanics	>50–250 kyr
Uranium series (^{230}Th/^{234}U)	245 kyr	Carbonates	<400 kyr
Thermoluminescence		Minerals	<500 kyr
Optically stimulated luminescence dating		Minerals	<400 kyr
Electron spin resonance		Tooth enamel, quartz	60 kyr to 2 myr
Cosmogenic nuclide (Al/Be)	1.36 myr*	Quartz	10 kyr to 10 myr

yr, years; kyr, thousand years; myr, million years; byr, billion years. *production rate ratio of ^{26}Al to ^{10}Be.

Table 2.1 Summary of some absolute dating methods commonly used in paleoanthropology, with half-lives (where relevant), materials dated, and applicable time ranges.

while it remains true that not every fossil or site can be chronometrically dated, advances made since the mid-twentieth century have ensured that by now the general chronology of human evolution is on a pretty secure footing. Table 2.1 summarizes the dating methods discussed and their characteristics.

Ancient Climates

Over the long haul, environmental stimuli appear to have been the most important drivers of evolutionary change, and during the history of the human subfamily the most significant sources of environmental change have been climatic. Climate not only directly impacts the physiological responses of organisms, but it also affects the local fauna and vegetation and thus the resources available even for the most opportunistic of omnivores. When a change in climate alters the vegetation and the animals you see around you, you do not have many choices. If you're not lucky enough to be able to move to a more congenial place, you will almost certainly go at least locally extinct. Adaptation in place will simply be too slow for the short timescales typically involved – although early members of our genus had the advantage of co-opting material culture to supply a degree of cushioning. At one end of the scale of effect, steep climatic changes have been associated with major faunal "turnovers"; at the other end, it is highly likely that constant buffeting by environmental change was in some way implicated in the extremely rapid evolution of the lineage that led to *Homo sapiens*.

Much of hominin evolution took place within the Pleistocene epoch, which was recently redefined as covering the past 2.58 myr. This was the time of the "Ice Ages," when high-latitude areas of the northern continents were periodically covered by gigantic ice sheets that swelled both southward, and down from mountain peaks, before retreating again. In the process they directly affected much of what is now the northern temperate zone, and more indirectly influenced climates in the subtropics and tropics that became more arid in cooler periods. All of this was imposed on a general long-term cooling of the oceans in response to the rearrangement of the continental masses due to tectonic drift, the coup de grâce coming when circulation of warmer waters between the Atlantic and Pacific oceans was finally entirely blocked off by the emergence of the Isthmus of Panama between North and South America at around 2.8 myr ago. For complex reasons, that event primed the conditions for ice cap formation in the northern hemisphere, as well as for further oceanic cooling. On the African continent such cooling was associated with increased seasonality of rainfall, and the consequent expansion of more open savanna formations. By shifting the focus from trees to grasses, those environmental changes made life possible for the vast herds of grazing animals that provided the crucial backdrop against which the hominins evolved.

Turning to (currently) temperate latitudes, a glacial landscape history such as the one left behind by the ice sheets on the northern continents poses a particular headache for geologists and geochronologists. That's because each ice sheet advance shifts and grinds away the rocky remnants of earlier events, and each melting episode releases vast quantities of running water to scour the terrain clean of the remaining evidence. Glacial episodes have therefore proven very difficult to reconstruct from traditional geological indications, and once more isotopes – this time stable isotopes of oxygen – have come to the rescue.

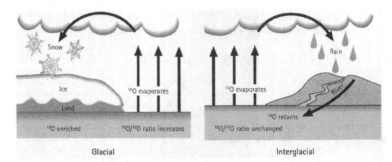

Figure 2.2   Oxygen isotopes in ice and seafloor cores. Past climates are reflected in the ratio of the oxygen isotopes ^{16}O and ^{18}O in the tests of tiny organisms recovered from cores taken from the ocean floor. The organisms derived these isotopes from the seawater in which they lived. The lighter ^{16}O evaporates preferentially from seawater and is returned to the sea in smaller quantities when precipitation becomes "locked up" in ice caps, so in colder times this isotope becomes rarer in seawater compared to ^{18}O.

Seawater contains two isotopes of oxygen: the heavier ^{18}O and the lighter and more abundant ^{16}O that evaporates more readily (Figure 2.2). Evaporated seawater is the source of most of the rain that falls, and in warmer times the light isotopes are returned to the sea as runoff and thus remain relatively abundant in seawater. But in cold times much of the rain gets "locked up" in the building ice caps that preferentially sequester ^{16}O, and the seas accordingly become relatively enriched in ^{18}O. The ratio between the two isotopes thus turns out to be a good proxy for prevailing temperatures; and it is, moreover, recorded not only in the accumulating ice sheets themselves, but in the carbonate "shells" of microscopic marine organisms that fall to the seafloor and become incorporated into the accumulating sediments. Using various kinds of calibration, temporal records of fluctuating temperatures can thus be constructed from changing isotopic ratios in cores drilled into the seabed, or into surviving ice sheets.

From isotopic data, paleoclimatologists have identified over 100 distinct "marine isotope stages" (MIS) over the span of the Pleistocene. These have been numbered backward, starting in the current warm stage, so that the warmer periods have been given odd numbers while the colder ones are even-numbered; higher-numbered stages are older than lower-numbered stages. Within each MIS there were minor fluctuations, some of them significant enough to have their own numeration, so that the warm Stage 5, for example, has five named substages. Among them, the very warm Stage 5e saw sea levels rise several meters above where they are currently, as the polar ice sheets melted and returned their water to the oceans. Conversely, during severely cold stages the ice sheets enlarged and sea levels dropped, exposing vast expanses of continental shelf (and hominid habitat) that are drowned today. At the beginning of the Pleistocene temperature oscillations were less pronounced than they became later, but were generally more frequent. As already noted, by about one million years ago they had settled down to a broadly 100 kyr cycle from one major peak of cold to the next, via a warmer interglacial and with many smaller excursions (sometimes amazingly short) in between.

It is not always easy to fit a particular hominid site directly to the isotopic sequences, but in combination with faunal, pollen, and soil studies and the palaeomagnetic record, those sequences have allowed us to tie many events in human evolution to the rich tapestry of environmental changes that continually altered the stage on which our evolution took place.

What Did They Eat?

Because you are quite literally what you eat, ancient diets are a big part of the human story, and scientists from many disciplines have accordingly devised ways of determining what they might have been. One early approach, now conducted with very sophisticated instrumentation, was to study how fossil teeth were worn in life, the nature and the hardness of the individual's diet determining how their chewing surfaces are grooved, pitted, and so forth. More recently the geochemists have gotten into the act, measuring the abundance in fossil bones and teeth of various stable isotopes that leave different chemical signatures according to their original owners' diets.

At the earlier end of the hominin time spectrum it is isotopes of carbon that are of interest. Most plants incorporate atmospheric carbon dioxide via what is called the C_3 pathway of photosynthesis, which leads to a low abundance of the stable ^{13}C isotope in the bones and teeth of the animals that feed on them. Some plants, however, fix carbon dioxide through the alternative C_4 pathway, resulting in a higher concentration of ^{13}C in the tissues. C_4 plants include the tropical savanna grasses on which grazing mammals typically feed; and the higher resulting levels of ^{13}C in those grazers additionally get transferred to the predators that hunt and feed on them. As a result, the relative abundance of these isotopes in its tissues will tell you what an ancient animal was eating, irrespective of its place in the food chain. Studies of this kind have revealed a surprisingly early taste for meat-eating in the hominin family.

Later in time, the isotopes of interest change to those of nitrogen, the most abundant gas in the atmosphere. The ratio in an animal's tissues between the stable isotopes ^{15}N and ^{14}N increases slightly with every step up the food chain: In general, the more meat you eat, the higher will be your level of ^{15}N. When some northern European Neanderthals were tested with this in mind, their fossils were found to have consistently higher ^{15}N/^{14}N ratios than those of herbivorous mammals from the same locality, ranking alongside wolves and hyenas. And in one case the ratio was so high that the researchers concluded that the hominins must have been eating herbivores that were exceptionally enriched in ^{15}N, reducing the potential menu to fearsome wooly mammoths and rhinoceros.

Interestingly, though, this does not mean that Neanderthals were highly carnivorous everywhere. In groundbreaking research published in 2010, some Neanderthals from the Middle East and from Europe were analyzed for the phytoliths embedded in the dental calculus that still adhered to their teeth. Phytoliths are tiny silicate mineral particles that form in plants, and they differ according to the plant concerned (and sometimes by plant part). And the calculus, of course, is the plaque nowadays removed by your dental hygienist at your annual checkup. The microscopic analysis of phytoliths revealed that at both Middle East and European sites a wide variety of plants had been consumed, reminding us that hominins are opportunistic omnivores whose food intake always responds to what is available in the environment. More recently, animal and plant DNA have also been isolated from dental calculus; and in 2020, using more traditional methods of analysis of archaeological remains, researchers found that, in the period around 100 kyr ago, Neanderthals at a coastal locality in Portugal were eating mussels, crabs, and local pine nuts. This reminds us that we usually get the most reliable picture when as many lines of evidence as possible are brought to bear on any question.

Virtual Reconstruction

Fossils rarely come out of the ground in pristine condition. In most cases they are broken and/or distorted, and in addition they are often encrusted by the sometimes extremely hard and tenaciously adhering matrix in which they have lain for hundreds of thousands or millions of years. The classic hominin example is the famous South African "Little Foot" skeleton. It took the paleontologist Ron Clarke 20 laborious years to free this important fossil from its underground prison via the laborious yet incredibly delicate physical removal of the surrounding rock – rock that was much harder than the bone it enclosed. But advances in technology now threaten to make such manual feats a thing of the past, or at least a major exception.

That is because, back in the 1980s, paleontologists began to adapt the novel clinical techniques of computerized axial tomography ("CT scanning") to their own use, often haunting hospitals in the wee hours to get precious free time on a clinical scanner. CT scanning basically involves taking numerous X-rays of parallel thin "slices" through an object, originally a human body, and then building them up using software into a three-dimensional view. In the early days, paleontologists would take CT images of their fossils, and then "digitally subtract" any adhering matrix. They would then inspect the interior detail revealed, before making a "stereolithograph" of the clean specimen using basically the same methods that 3D printers use today. But it was soon realized that the technology was capable of much more than this, especially as the resolution of the images improved and huge advances were made in the software for manipulating them. Nowadays a fossil can be imaged in an industrial machine that emits much more radiation than a hospital CT scanner would ever be allowed to, and that will give you a correspondingly more refined image of all its surfaces. That image can then be imported into a computer, and subsequently manipulated onscreen in any way you might want.

One popular application is in reconstruction. Badly cracked and distorted fossils can be extremely difficult to physically prepare without damaging them even more. But nowadays a bowling-ball of a broken and fragile fossil skull, held together by tough and heavy matrix, can be placed into a scanner as is and have its matrix digitally removed. The image can then be imported into a computer, and the skull's individual pieces separated and reassembled on the computer screen by a knowledgeable (and very patient) operator. Once the reconstruction is done, an impression of the brain that had dwelled within can be "virtually" extracted from the now-undistorted interior of the braincase, its volume precisely measured, and its details recorded. Finally, both skull and brain can be printed out for further study. In this way, a procedure that would have taken months at best, and that might even have placed the original fossil at risk, can be completed in days or weeks. Excitingly, even such tiny features as the bones of the middle ear can now be digitally extracted and studied in exquisite detail.

One offshoot of such imaging techniques is the study of the internal structures of the bones and teeth themselves, which can now be done in extreme detail by using scanners attached to particle accelerators that bring enormous energy to the imaging process. A particularly intriguing application of this technology has been the study of the development of teeth in ancient juveniles, in which the finest of growth increments can now be observed – even the lines that indicate the moment of weaning! We human beings are remarkable for the long periods we spend as helpless infants and growing up as juveniles – which is, of course, when we learn the many things that are necessary for us to know to function properly within our complicated societies. Accordingly, as adults we are largely the people we have learned to be. These new imaging techniques hold immense promise for future understanding of exactly how and when our species acquired its long and specialized learning trajectory.

Genomics

The recognition in the 1940s that the DNA residing in the chromosomes of everyone's cells was the molecule of heredity, and the discovery in 1953 of the molecule's double-helical structure, paved the way for the genomic technology that has since found an integral place in paleoanthropology. DNA not only encodes population histories that can be deciphered from its sequence, but also specifies the information needed for the synthesis of structural and functional molecules, and thus tells you a lot about any individual organism from which you can extract it. There are three paleoanthropological contexts in which DNA has proven particularly relevant: the determination of the precise position that we human beings occupy among the great apes that are our closest living relatives; tracing exactly how a tiny population of *Homo sapiens* living somewhere in Africa contrived eventually to colonize the entire world; and better understanding our extinct relatives who lived within the last several hundred thousand years – the period within which, under favorable conditions, fragments of the fragile DNA may be preserved.

The DNA molecules of which the chromosomes are made consist of long chains of chemical units, known as "nucleotides," that can be of four kinds: A, C, G, and T. Two chains are joined to each other to form the famous double-helix (rather like a twisted ladder); and pairs of chains are complementary in structure, because an A in one chain will only join with a T in the other, and a G with a C. That means that the two strands are reverse-images of each other, running in opposite directions. What the early geneticists referred to as "genes" are stretches of nucleotides, defined by "punctuation" sequences, that specify the proteins from which each new individual will be constructed. "Regulatory" sequences can also turn such "structural" genes on and off, and thereby modify the developmental processes that lead to the phenotype. There are some three billion bases in the human genome, most of them appearing not to code for proteins. To date, it remains unknown what many of the noncoding sequences do, though some of this "junk" codes for noncoding RNAs, molecules that in turn help regulate the activity of protein-coding genes.

To cut a very long story short, gene mutations are the copying errors that are occasionally introduced when the DNA is replicated as new cells are formed. The random substitution of an A for a G, or a C for a T, for instance, creates what is known as a "single nucleotide polymorphism" (SNP), a new variant that may or may not materially alter the effects of the gene. As a result, mutations may be advantageous or disadvantageous to individuals possessing them, or alternatively their effects may be entirely neutral. In all cases, though, a new SNP can be a "witness" to a history that it will write into the DNA of subsequent generations. Single nucleotide polymorphisms are ideally structured for quantitative analysis, and databases are now available for large numbers of individuals around the world.

As noted, DNA is a long and fragile molecule. It is packaged into the paired chromosomes that each of us has in the nuclei of our cells, one of each pair from each parent. During life the molecule's integrity is maintained by an intricate protein apparatus, but following cell death it rapidly breaks apart into smaller and smaller pieces. In hot and humid surroundings DNA rapidly disintegrates beyond hope of reconstruction; even in colder and drier places, after about 40 kyr (taking us back to the latest Neanderthals) it is reduced to tiny fragments. However, as it happens, so-called "next-generation" techniques of rapid DNA sequencing deliberately sever DNA of interest into easily sequenced smaller fragments before piecing it together using computer algorithms. As a result, those techniques are in some cases perfect for reconstituting the severely fragmented DNA of Neanderthals and early *Homo sapiens*. Complete genomes are now available for a handful of Neanderthal individuals and several dozen early *H. sapiens*. The most ancient piece of hominin bone from which DNA has been extracted thus far is about 430 kyr old.

The constant mixing that occurs as maternal and paternal DNA are combined from one generation to the next complicates analysis, but two human DNA systems are "clonally inherited." One of them is the small DNA fraction that is contained outside the cell's nucleus in the mitochondria, the tiny organelles that are the "powerhouses" of almost every cell in our bodies; the other is the DNA of the Y chromosomes that only the males among us possess. The mitochondrial DNA (mtDNA) is passed along solely through the maternal line because, although it does pass from mother to son, it stops there because any mitochondria in the filial sperm are prohibited from entering the fertilized egg. And the DNA of the small Y chromosome is, of course, paternally inherited because only males have Y chromosomes. In both cases, then, we are dealing with simplified inheritance systems in which differences accumulated over time are due strictly to mutation rather than being complicated by biparental recombination. It turns out that some parts of the small circular mitochondrial genome tend to change fast, while others change much more slowly; but a clear advantage for paleogenomicists is that thousands of mitochondria exist in a typical cell that contains only one chromosome of each kind. The upshot is that mtDNA is much more plentiful in most tissues than Y chromosome DNA, and so is more likely to be preserved in recoverable form.

The first worldwide comparative analysis of human SNPs focused on mtDNA, and a lot of subsequent work has permitted scientists to recognize numerous distinct and geographically linked human "haplogroups" in both mitochondrial and Y chromosome DNA sets (the term derives from the "haploid" nature of unpaired uniparental DNA, in contrast to "diploid," which refers to the paired DNA). Those haplogroups were given alphabetical letters in the order of their discovery, and subgroups were added as necessary. From early on it was evident that all mtDNA and Y chromosome haplotypes converge back in time to single lineages that lived in Africa; and haplotype markers of both kinds have proven to be very useful instruments for reconstructing subsequent human population movements around the world.

3 Discovery and Interpretation of the Human Fossil Record: The Early Days

In the Beginning: *Homo neanderthalensis*

When Charles Darwin published *On the Origin of Species* in 1859, only a tiny handful of human fossils – the material evidence of the ancient human history that his book implied must exist – had been discovered. Some of them had not even yet been properly recognized, although the most significant of them – the partial skeleton from the Neander Valley in Germany that had recently been found alongside the remains of extinct Ice Age animals – was on the brink of becoming the world's most famous fossil. Discovered accidentally in 1856 by lime miners, and only preserved by great good chance, the Neanderthal skeleton – principally a large skullcap (Figure 3.1, right) and some very robust limb bones – rapidly became the subject of vigorous debate in Germany between those who thought it had belonged to a member of an ancient barbarous tribe, and those who thought it simply the remains of a pathological modern human. In England it caught the attention of the comparative anatomist Thomas Henry Huxley, an expert on dinosaurs who had been Darwin's most vociferous supporter following the publication of the *Origin*, but who had also chided him for rejecting the notion that Nature at least occasionally "makes jumps" (i.e., speciates).

The idea may have been as unfamiliar as it was uncomfortable that, like all other vertebrates, humans must have fossil relatives; but nobody in the world was better positioned than Huxley to recognize that the unfamiliar Neanderthaler represented an ancient, distinctive, and now-extinct kind of human. For even though it had originally contained a brain as large as that of a modern person, the Neanderthal skull itself was very different from our own: it was thick, and

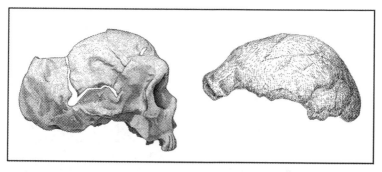

Figure 3.1   The first two crania of *Homo neanderthalensis* discovered: Gibraltar (left) and Neanderthal (right). Not to exact scale.

very long, and very low; it protruded at the back; and it was adorned in front with prominent brow ridges that arced gracefully above each eye. By the standards undoubtedly familiar to the experienced anatomist that Huxley was, it amply justified the recognition of a new species, albeit somehow related to *Homo sapiens*. Yet in his 1863 essay collection, *Man's Place in Nature*, Huxley tied himself in knots explaining how the Neanderthal fossil simply represented "the extreme term of a series gradually leading from it to the highest and best-developed of human crania." In other words, it was simply a brutish *Homo sapiens*.

What a lost opportunity! Because, however convenient and congenial it might have been, this conclusion had no basis whatever in the Darwinian logic that Huxley had so vigorously defended. Instead, his reasoning clearly, and with the deepest irony, reflected the "Great Chain of Being" concept that harked back to Aristotle and the medieval Christian Scholastics – and from which Darwin's ideas had offered the best prospect of escape. If the Neanderthal individual had belonged to any subfamily other than the human one, Huxley would almost certainly have concluded that it belonged to its own distinctive species. But, in the end, he fell prey to the constantly gnawing human excep-tionalism that has plagued paleoanthropology ever since. Because there is only one hominin in the world today, the default supposition is that there has only ever been one, our ancestors disappearing back into the past in a thin, unbranching chain. So the big brain of the Neanderthaler meant that the fossil was one of us, whatever it might have looked like.

Just for the record, it seems that Darwin himself was content with this capitulation to convention. He waited more than a decade after publishing the *Origin* to make his own statement, in the two-volume *Descent of Man* that was published in 1871; and even then, while willing to speculate at length about how a purely hypothetical ancient and upright human ancestor might have emerged in Africa using its freed-up hands to wield tools, he gave the actual human fossil record a wide berth. He merely noted that the Neanderthal fossil showed that you could be ancient and still have a big brain. What that might have meant he failed to specify, though he didn't bother to contradict the Galway anatomist William King, who in 1863 had placed the Neanderthal cranium in its own species *Homo neanderthalensis* and, noting its lack of a lofty forehead, had hazarded that "the thoughts and desires that once dwelt within it never soared beyond those of the brute."

Perhaps the most curious aspect of Darwin's reluctance to confront the few human fossils then known, in a book in which one might have expected them to feature front and center, was that he had actually held a Neanderthal skull in his hands – which, as any paleoanthropologist will tell you, is a very powerful experience. In 1864, the paleontologist Hugh Falconer had brought him a Neanderthal skull that had been recently discovered in Gibraltar (Figure 3.1, left). Darwin had certainly stared into its vacant orbits, and his agile brain must have been flooded with thoughts and feelings. But of what? All he recorded of the fossil was that it was "wonderful." As indeed it was, as a fairly complete cranium that, unlike the original Neanderthaler, included the face. Its particular importance at the time, however, was to demonstrate that the Neanderthal fossil had been no freak: The two specimens, discovered hundreds of miles apart, had entirely comparable morphologies. But, sadly, this did not provoke any immediate rethinking. George Busk, the anatomist who described the Gibraltar cranium, thought that, as "low and savage" as its braincase might have been, the skull was still that of a "man, and not a halfway step between man and monkey."

Further supporting evidence for the characteristic Neanderthal morphology was not to come for two long decades; but in 1886, excavations at the cave of

Spy in Belgium finally produced two Neanderthal skeletons in association with what we now call "Mousterian" tools – sophisticated stone implements made on flakes struck from carefully prepared "cores," of a kind already well known from European Ice Age sites (Figure 7.3). The Mousterian had already been situated by the French prehistorian Gabriel de Mortillet in a "Palaeolithic," or "Old Stone Age," sequence of "cultures" that were recognized from distinctive tool types. It lay toward the bottom (older) end of the sequence, just above the basal "Acheulean" that was characterized by the "handaxe," a large, teardrop-shaped tool (Figure 6.2) made by removing flakes from a stone "nucleus" using a stone (later, softer) "hammer." Above the Mousterian in Mortillet's scheme lay in sequence the Aurignacian, Gravettian, and Magdalenian cultures, all now known to be the handiwork of fully modern human hunter-gatherers. These were soon followed by the Neolithic "New Stone Age," the product of early farmers who finished their stone axes by polishing them. The Spy cave also contained abundant remains of ancient mammals – mammoth, wooly rhino, and so on – which confirmed that the Neanderthals dated from somewhere in the succession of "Ice Ages" that geologists already knew had affected Europe in the geologically relatively recent past. At the time, nobody knew exactly what that meant in years, though the Spy skeletons are now reckoned to be around 40 kyr old. But what the Belgian find most importantly meant, as the nineteenth century neared its end, was that in the minds of many the Neanderthals now had an identity as a distinctive human relative. Big-brained, but strongly built and with a long, low cranial vault and strongly jutting face, that relative had lived during the Ice Ages – during which it was already known that modern humans had also been on the landscape – and had made stone tools with great skill.

Pithecanthropus erectus

In the year following the Spy discovery, a young Dutch anatomist embarked on a voyage to the Dutch East Indies with the explicit aim of finding the remains of ancient tropical humans. And in 1891 Eugene Dubois miraculously realized that ambition, when a work gang under his direction exhumed a skullcap (Figure 3.2, left) on the banks of Java's Solo River, at a locality called Trinil that faunal remains suggested was much older than anything known from Europe. The cranium was even flatter than the Neanderthal

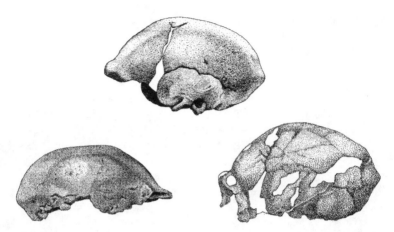

Figure 3.2   *Homo erectus* skullcaps from Trinil (left), Sangiran (center), and Zhoukoudian (right). Not to exact scale.

one, and at 940 ml the brain it had contained was markedly small (modern humans now average 1,330 ml; both Neanderthals and Pleistocene *Homo sapiens* averaged about 1,500 ml). At first, Dubois considered his fossil brain-case to be chimpanzee-like (though chimp brains average about 400 ml); but in the next year his crew came up with a well-mineralized femur (thighbone) that, apart from a pathological excrescence, was indistinguishable from a modern one. This changed his mind; in 1894 Dubois published his finds under the name of *Pithecanthropus erectus* (meaning upright ape-man). He saw his new species as part of a series that began not with the chimpanzees, but with the gibbons, the lesser apes of the East Indies, and that ended in *Homo sapiens* (which for him included the Neanderthals). And as far as he was concerned, his new specimen was neither human nor ape: His life reconstruction, preserved in the natural history museum of Leiden, shows an upright but beetle-browed and long-waisted human, with long hands (one of them clutching a pointed bone) and semi-grasping feet with somewhat divergent great toes.

When he returned to Holland, Dubois soon found himself scooped by the German anatomist Gustav Schwalbe, who quickly published a monograph on

Pithecanthropus in which he placed it at the beginning of a slowly evolving lineage that transformed into *Homo sapiens* via *Homo neanderthalensis* (which he called *Homo primigenius* – by dint of new discoveries, the Neanderthals were beginning to gather names). Annoyed, Dubois retired from the fray, and at least for the moment Schwalbe's strictly linear version of human evolution triumphed unopposed. Given how little was known at the time, and the power of Darwin's gradualist ideas, that version was reasonable enough. But it is also important to remember that it was in the context of an extremely impoverished human fossil record that *Pithecanthropus erectus*, a hominin found in a far-flung geographical dead-end, became established both in the paleoanthropological mind and public perception as the direct progenitor of today's humankind.

The Early Twentieth Century

During the 1890s and the following decade several important Neanderthal discoveries were made, mainly in France but also as far to the east as Croatia (Figure 3.3, left). Advances in geology had also confirmed that the Neanderthals had been the aboriginal inhabitants of Europe, only later joined there by the incoming early modern humans known informally as "Cro-Magnons." Schwalbe's linear scheme was thus appearing vindicated, at least until the Parisian anatomist Marcellin Boule intervened. Between 1911 and 1913, Boule published sections of a highly influential monograph on the deliberately

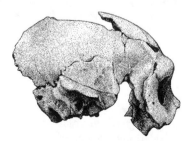
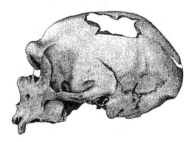

Figure 3.3   Neanderthal crania from Krapina, Croatia (left) and La Chapelle-aux-Saints, France (right). Not to scale.

buried and beautifully preserved skeleton of an aged male Neanderthal that had been excavated from a small cave at La Chapelle-aux-Saints in south-central France (Figure 3.3, right). And he arrived at an unequivocal conclusion: *Homo neanderthalensis* was an evolutionary dead-end, abruptly replaced in Europe by the incoming and immeasurably more sophisticated *Homo sapiens.* In arriving at what seems in retrospect a reasonable taxonomic judgment, Boule unfortunately launched a thousand mocking cartoons by painting an unflattering and inaccurate, but enormously influential, portrait of a shambling biped with a hunched neck, bent knees, apelike grasping big toes, and a brain that, although large, was of inferior quality. Intriguingly, Boule barely bothered to mention *Pithecanthropus*, dismissing it in passing as a giant gibbon. His preferred candidate for human ancestor was *Eoanthropus dawsoni.*

Who was *Eoanthropus* (dawn man)? Well, in 1908 a lawyer named Charles Dawson reported finding some thick fragments of human skull at a place in southern England called Piltdown. Excavations of the site by Arthur Smith Woodward, Keeper of Geology at what is now the London Natural History Museum, turned up further cranial and lower jaw fragments and a short canine tooth, in association with artifacts and some mammal fossils of pre-Pleistocene age. These were the fossils Smith Woodward described as *Eoanthropus*; and soon the handful of anatomists who made up the London paleoanthropological establishment were all in on the act. Despite some internecine squabbles, they agreed that the fossils were those of an ancient and thick-skulled human precursor that had possessed a large brain and reduced canine, in combination with an apelike lower jaw that lacked a chin. That combination sat comfortably with an assumed "brain first" model of human evolution that viewed the large brain as modern humankind's most remarkable feature, and thus as the most foundational. The only problem was that the "fossil" was fraudulent. It was a chimera of a human braincase and an ape jaw that had been suitably broken, colored, and filed down to disguise the discrepancies between them. Though some suspected at the time that the ape and human fragments were not associated, the fraud was only officially revealed in 1952; and in the meantime, the scam served to mislead many observers such as Boule. Mostly, though, it gave rise to a mini-industry of speculation about the identity of the fraudster; and although figures as disparate as the theologian Pierre Teilhard de Chardin and the novelist

Arthur Conan Doyle have been implicated, the only common factor in all scenarios is Charles Dawson who, it turns out, was a practiced and thoroughly shameless trickster.

More productively, 1908 was also the year when the German prehistorian Otto Schoetensack found a distinctive hominid lower jaw in a quarry at a village called Mauer, near Heidelberg. Since the associated fauna looked very archaic, and the jaw itself didn't look like that of a Neanderthal, Schoetensack gave it its own name, *Homo heidelbergensis*. For his part, Boule wrote it off as a Neanderthal ancestor, and only recently has its full importance been appreciated. Boule's disparaging interpretation of the Neanderthals ruled until 1927, when the Hungarian-American physician Aleš Hrdlička lectured London's Royal Anthropological Institute about "The Neanderthal Phase of Man." His title says it all: Neanderthals were directly ancestral to modern humans and, rather than being replaced by Cro-Magnons, had evolved into them. Hrdlička saw the considerable anatomical variation within the rapidly accumulating sample of Neanderthal fossils as the result of adaptive modification with time, a view that seemed to be borne out by Arthur Smith Woodward's interpretation of a skull discovered in Zambia in 1921 (Figure 7.1, center) as an intermediate between Neanderthals and *Homo sapiens*. This beautiful fossil was, however, rapidly upstaged by another discovery in southern Africa.

Australopithecus and Peking Man

In early 1925 the Australian neuroanatomist Raymond Dart, Professor of Anatomy at Witwatersrand University Medical School in Johannesburg, published a description of a newly discovered skull (Figure 3.4) of what he considered a very ancient human precursor, under the title of "*Australopithecus africanus*: The Ape-Man of South Africa." The specimen concerned had been blasted out of a lime mine at a place called Taung, some 270 miles to the southwest. The mine had also yielded the remains of long-extinct baboon species, so Dart guessed that the child was seriously old, whatever that might mean. He was right: The skull is now believed to have fallen, some 2.8 myr ago, from an eagle's nest into the underground cavity from which it was retrieved. The rather odd name he chose for it – *Australopithecus africanus* – translates as "southern ape of Africa."

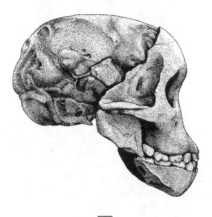

Figure 3.4   Side and front views of the infant cranium from Taung, South Africa.

The skull itself was that of a very young individual in whom the first molar had just erupted (which happens in *Homo sapiens* at the age of six). The little face was attached to a natural cast of the brain which, at 440 ml in volume, was very small, barely bigger than that of a chimpanzee. Nobody had ever seen the combination of characteristics this fossil presented; but evidently the skull had belonged either to an ape with some humanlike features, or to a rather apelike human or prehuman. Deciding which, was complicated by the fact that juvenile apes and humans resemble each other very much more than adults do; but Dart came down on the human side. He pointed particularly to what he saw as some presaging of the human condition in the "higher centres" of the brain, and to the fact that upright posture (the second great distinguishing feature of humankind, along with the large brain) was suggested by the placement beneath the skull of the foramen magnum, the large hole through which the spinal cord exits the brain. His conclusion was that the Taung child possessed "just those characters that are to be expected in an extinct link between man and his simian ancestor" (while, just for the record, *Pithecanthropus* was "a caricature of precocious hominid failure").

None of this went down very well with the grandees of paleoanthropology in London, where Dart's paper had appeared, unheralded, in the prestigious journal *Nature*. Dart had studied in London and was known to all; but he was nonetheless a colonial outsider, and four invited expert responses in *Nature* ranged from the lukewarm to the downright derogatory (the least favorable of them coming from Smith Woodward, still in thrall to Piltdown). This was maybe to be expected, especially since none of the commentators had seen anything but muddy pictures of the fossil. What was maybe more surprising was the public reaction: One newspaper reader hoped to see Dart "in an institution for the feebleminded," while another wrote from France predicting that he would "roast in the quenchless fires of Hell." Discouraged, Dart withdrew from the paleoanthropological fray and turned his attention to less fraught matters. He didn't bring his fossil to Europe for his colleagues to see until six years later, when attitudes against it had hardened.

By this time paleoanthropological attention had also been diverted east, to China. Between 1929 and 1934, excavators at a cave site now known as Zhoukoudian, on the outskirts of Beijing, recovered a trove of hominin fossils that included 14 partial skulls, mainly braincases with volumes between 850 and 1,200 ml (Figure 3.2, right; illustrated individual 1,030 ml). Although they showed extensive similarities to Eugene Dubois's Trinil skullcap, they were given their own name: *Sinanthropus pekinensis*. Davidson Black, the Canadian anatomist in charge, also reported that some of the associated animal bones had been charred, suggesting that Peking Man had mastered the use of fire. Following his death in 1934, Black was replaced by the German anatomist Franz Weidenreich, an early doubter of Piltdown who had studied Neanderthals in his home country, and who went on to document the Peking Man fossils in a series of magnificent monographs. Weidenreich also accounted for the extensive breakage of the hominin bones found at Zhoukoudian by suggesting that *Sinanthropus* had been a cannibal – something that it later turned out was not that unusual among extinct *Homo* species, although it also turned out that the broken bones from Zhoukoudian were better explained by hyena activity. Similarly, it later transpired that far from being evidence of campfires, the "charring" that Black had noted was actually natural staining by manganese.

Work at Zhoukoudian had to be suspended in 1937 in the face of the Japanese invasion, and in the next year Weidenreich was forced to flee to New York.

A later attempt to ship the hominid fossils to him for safety led to their tragic disappearance amid the chaos of war. But before leaving the region, Weidenreich had visited Ralph von Koenigswald, a German-Dutch geologist who was working in Java, and who had been instrumental in the recovery there of more *Pithecanthropus* specimens in the Sangiran region (Figure 3.2, center). As late as 1938, an anonymous commentator in *Nature* had been able to write that, "of recent years, opinion has tended to an increasing degree to incline" to the view that Dubois's *Pithecanthropus* was an ape rather than human; but von Koenigswald's discoveries confirmed their human identity, and the two researchers agreed on the close similarities between the Javanese and Chinese forms, although they thought that the former had existed earlier in time.

Once ensconced in New York at the American Museum of Natural History, Weidenreich developed a theory to account for the diversity of peoples in the world today, even though members of different geographical groups readily breed with each other. He envisaged deep roots for the modern geographic groups – Javanese fossil hominids had, for example, given rise to today's "Australian group," while *Sinanthropus* was the ancestor of the "Mongolian group" – although the integrity of the species was maintained by interbreeding among those lineages. As he eventually admitted, this schema required that "all primate forms recognized as hominids – no matter whether they lived in the past or live today – represent morphologically a unity when compared with other primate forms and they can be regarded as *one species*" (his emphasis). This was a judgment no systematist could or would ever make (it's equivalent to saying that lions, jaguars, and house cats are all one species, just because they are all not dogs); but, as we will see, it would return to haunt paleoanthropology.

Back in South Africa, a country physician and paleontologist called Robert Broom had been inspired by Raymond Dart's discovery to look for more early hominins in the lime mines of the Johannesburg region. Those mines were places on the eroding landscape where formerly subterranean accumulations of bones and rock fragments were exposed, along with the interspersed flowstones that the miners wanted for their kilns. Broom knew that baboon fossils were found in such places: Why not hominins? In 1936, he hit paydirt when a rather battered skull turned up at the Sterkfontein mine. Calling his find

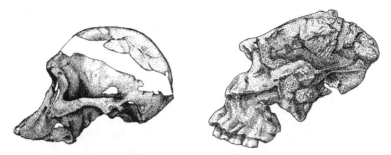

Figure 3.5 A gracile australopith cranium (Sts 5) from Sterkfontein (left) and a robust counterpart (SK 46) from Swartkrans, South Africa (right). Not to exact scale.

Plesianthropus transvaalensis (near-man of the Transvaal) because he believed it to be a bit younger than Dart's fossil, he redoubled his efforts and in 1938 found fossils of a generally similar but more massively built hominid at the nearby Kromdraai mine. This one he called *Paranthropus robustus* (robust next-to-man), and it was soon to be joined by the allied *Paranthropus crassidens* from the Swartkrans mine, not far away. Both the lightly built ("gracile") and "robust" forms (Figure 3.5, left and right, respectively) had evidently had small brains and large faces, in combination with reduced canine teeth. But the robust type had smaller incisors and larger chewing teeth, all housed in a very heavily built skull. Right after he'd found the latter, Broom was visited by the distinguished American Museum paleontologist William King Gregory and his dentist colleague Milo Hellman, both of whom concurred that his fossils of both kinds were "in both a structural and a genetic sense the conservative cousins of the contemporary human branch." Their hominin status was now attested by independent international experts.

Many more such "australopith" fossils duly showed up, including bones of the skeleton that confirmed upright locomotion. This emboldened Dart to get back into the act, and he began work at the Makapansgat limeworks in the northern Transvaal, a site that eventually yielded numerous hominid fossils. These were probably older than those from further south (some may be as old as 3 myr, compared to around 2.6 to 2.0 myr for the bulk of the Sterkfontein fossils, and under 2 myr for Kromdraai and Swartkrans). From the latter, Broom and his younger associate John Robinson eventually also reported finding some very lightly built fossils that they called *Telanthropus capensis* ("far man from the Cape"), suggesting that this species might be "intermediate between one of the ape-men and true man." Nowadays those fossils, along with others from late levels at Sterkfontein, are usually referred to our own genus *Homo*. While all this was going on, the British establishment remained aloof and distinctly unimpressed, until the distinguished anatomist Wilfrid LeGros Clark finally gave the australopiths his imprimatur following a visit to South Africa in 1947. Capitulation was rapid; by 1950 the australopiths were (almost) universally accepted as representatives of the earliest known phase of hominin evolution.

The australopiths had small brains, mostly in the 400–500 ml range. But did they use tools? Raymond Dart thought so. As at Zhoukoudian, the animal and human bones from Makapansgat were all broken, and some were blackened (which is why Dart called the hominins *Australopithecus prometheus*, because he thought they had used fire). Letting his imagination rip, Dart attributed the smashed-up animal and human remains at Makapansgat to the butchery and cooking activities of the australopiths, who had used bones as hammers, teeth as saws, and horn cores as daggers, hence wielding an "osteodontokeratic" (bone, tooth, horn) material culture. Mankind, it seemed, was born of "murderers and flesh hunters," an origin that had inevitably led to "the blood-spattered, slaughter-gutted archives of mankind." A fine dramatic story, and one that was dramatized by Robert Ardrey in his bestselling *African Genesis* and brought to the screen by Stanley Kubrick in his classic movie *2001: A Space Odyssey*. Its only flaw lay in being completely mistaken. The bone accumulations at Makapansgat turned out to be the work of humble porcupines; and the vulnerable, small-bodied australopiths, bereft of the dagger-like canine teeth of their remote ancestors, had most likely been the hunted, not the hunters.

The Synthesis Arrives in Paleoanthropology

You won't have failed to notice that most of the paleoanthropologists mentioned so far were physicians or human anatomists by trade. And while it certainly made intuitive sense that an anatomist should be the go-to expert when anyone found the remains of an ancient hominin, it is also important to

realize that human anatomists were trained to document the intimate variations of human structure, rather than to understand and organize the rich
variety of organisms among which human beings belong, or to discover the
intricacies of evolutionary histories. You will, for instance, scour the index of
Arthur Keith's 1915 classic *The Antiquity of Man* in vain for any mention
of such subjects as biological diversity or natural selection. Among other areas
of ignorance, the anatomists in question knew – and cared – little about the
rules that govern the nomenclature of animal species and genera. Instead, they
looked on zoological names as no more than convenient identifiers, roughly
equivalent to their own family and given names. This inevitably spawned
a plethora of genus and species names that gave a spurious impression of
hominin variety.

The first person to publicly deplore this tendency was Theodosius Dobzhansky,
the geneticist who had masterminded the Modern Evolutionary Synthesis. With
brisk confidence for one who had probably never seen a human fossil,
Dobzhansky quite correctly informed paleoanthropologists in 1944 that their
typological approach had given a false idea of "a tree with many branches." But
he then went over the top, declaring that everything that had happened in
human evolution since the time of Java Man had occurred within a single
variable species, thereby both supporting Weidenreich's notions of simultan-
eous divergence and integration and setting the stage for the unrealistically
broad view of hominin taxa that lingers today. Still, as World War II was raging
nobody had much time to listen, and it was left to Dobzhansky's fellow prophet
of the Synthesis, Ernst Mayr, to drop the real bombshell once peace had
returned.

In 1950 Mayr – an ornithologist, remember – addressed the assembled good
and great of paleoanthropology at a conference held at the Cold Spring Harbor
Biological Laboratory, on New York's Long Island. He castigated them for
their poor grasp of biological process, and he minced no words in informing
them that an unjustified profusion of names in paleoanthropology had produced a gravely misleading picture of high past hominin diversity. Instead,
human evolution had proceeded as a simple progression of species, within
a single though variable lineage that was entirely embraced by the genus
Homo. *Homo transvaalensis* (the australopiths) had evolved gradually into
Homo erectus (Java and Peking), which in turn had transformed smoothly into

Homo sapiens (including Neanderthals). The human family, Mayr airily declared, had "specialized in despecialization," and he forcefully reiterated Dobzhansky's earlier theme that the human ecological niche was so broad that only one human species could ever have existed at any one point in time. The audience was gobsmacked. Guiltily aware that they had been operating in a theoretical vacuum all along, its older members went into a state of shock; and some of the younger ones were inspired to initiate a "New Physical Anthropology" in which adaptation and natural selection reigned supreme, and systematics barely figured at all.

Remarkably enough, in the immediate aftermath of Mayr's broadside only one contrary voice was raised. John Robinson objected from far-away South Africa that the robust and gracile australopiths proved that multiple hominin lineages could exist simultaneously, a point that Mayr himself grudgingly but rapidly conceded. Nonetheless, in the new minimalist spirit most writers began subsuming all australopiths into the single genus *Australopithecus*, although more recently the robust ones have reasserted their identity as *Paranthropus*.

Mayr's intervention changed paleoanthropology permanently, both for the better and for the worse. On the one hand, the breaking of the anatomists' authoritarian grip not only cleared away a lot of taxonomic clutter, but also allowed the biological anthropologists who largely succeeded them to broaden the study of human evolution in salutary ways inspired by the Synthesis. Questions of adaptation, function, distribution, and environment came to the fore as researchers sought to paint more complete pictures of the lives of departed hominins. On the other hand, paleoanthropologists became extraordinarily shy of using zoological names; even today, an associated reluctance to recognize new species makes it impossible to properly appreciate the historical complexities of the hominin story. This is a serious deficiency because, while intraspecies processes are undoubtedly important, it is species that are the principal actors in the evolutionary drama; and if you don't accurately identify the actors, you'll never properly understand the play.

Exemplary of the postwar generation of paleoanthropologists was the University of Chicago's F. Clark Howell, who began publishing on the Neanderthals just before the Piltdown "fossil" was officially put to rest in

1952. Unencumbered by *Eoanthropus*, Howell identified a continuous western European lineage that began with the Mauer jaw and continued through a couple of crania that had been discovered at Steinheim in Germany (Figure 7.4, right) and Swanscombe in England. Next came the "early Neanderthals" from sites in Italy (Figure 7.5, right) and Germany, and the series culminated in the "classic" Neanderthals such as Boule's La Chapelle individual (Figure 3.3, right). In the east, Howell envisaged a separate lineage that began with lightly built Neanderthals from Eastern Europe (Figure 3.3, left), and ultimately gave rise to modern humans via a rather enigmatic form represented at Mont Carmel, in Israel. Modern humans from the east had then spread westwards to oust their relatives, the classic Neanderthals. This busy evolutionary activity had involved a lot of local natural selection, but its overall pattern had been mediated by dramatic Ice Age oscillations in climate that had isolated eastern from western Europe at one moment and united them the next. There was an immediacy and freshness in Howell's account that was missing from the prewar literature (maybe apart from some of Dart's more lurid contributions); and, since it was implicit that everything had taken place within the bounds of a single species, there was no need for the zoological names that were conspicuous by their absence from Howell's scenario.

Paleoanthropology also saw its first absolute dates during the 1950s, when the Harvard University archaeologist Hallam Movius applied the novel radiocarbon dating method to late Paleolithic sites in southwestern France. With some subsequent fine-tuning, it turned out that Mortillet's Aurignacian culture had appeared at over 40 kyr ago, as the first modern humans trickled into Europe, and that it had given way to the Gravettian at about 28 kyr ago. The subsequent Solutrean culture (added since Mortillet's time) began at around 22 kyr ago, and the Magdalenian, the final phase of the Upper Paleolithic, ran from about 18 kyr to 11 kyr. The Mousterian culture of the Neanderthals still lies largely beyond the reach of early radiocarbon dating, but there are not many convincing dates for it under about 40 kyr. Since Movius's pioneering work, radiocarbon chronology has remained central to the archaeology of the late Paleolithic, even as other methods of absolute dating (Chapter 2) have become available.

Table 3.1 summarizes the hominin species discussed in this chapter.

Original Name	Current Name	Named By	Date	Where Found	Age
Homo neanderthalensis	*H. neanderthalensis*	W. King	1863	Germany	40 kyr
Pithecanthropus erectus	*H. erectus*	E. Dubois	1892	Java	>700 kyr
Eoanthropus dawsoni	n/a (fake)	A. Woodward	1913	England	n/a
Australopithecus africanus	*A. africanus*	R. Dart	1925	South Africa	~2.8 myr
Sinanthropus pekinensis	*H. erectus*	D. Black	1927	China	~600 kyr
Plesianthropus t'vaalensis	*A. africanus*	R. Broom	1936	South Africa	~2.4 myr
Paranthropus robustus	*P. robustus*	R. Broom	1938	South Africa	~2.0 myr
Australopithecus p'theus	*A. prometheus*	R. Dart	1948	South Africa	<3.0 myr
Telanthropus capensis	*H. ergaster*	J. Robinson	1953	South Africa	1.9 myr

kyr, thousand years; myr, million years; t'vaalensis = *transvaalensis*; p'theus = *prometheus*.

Table 3.1 Summary of the principal hominin species discussed in this chapter, in order of description, with the name originally given, by whom named, and the name by which the species is known currently (by this author). Date is that of original publication, and age and locality are those of the type specimen.

4 Discovery and Interpretation of the Human Fossil Record: Later Developments

East Africa: *Zinjanthropus boisei* and *Homo habilis*

The next major entrant into the field of postwar paleoanthropology was Louis Leakey, a flamboyant character who had been scouring his East African homeland for hominid fossils since the 1930s. One major site of interest, in what is now Tanzania, was a large erosional gulley called Olduvai Gorge. And in 1959, in the Gorge's oldest exposed sediments (known as Bed I), Louis's archaeologist wife, Mary, discovered the cranium of a hyper-robust australopith that had tiny incisors and canines, and huge, flat cheek teeth (Figure 4.1, right). In the same year Louis named this amazing specimen *Zinjanthropus boisei* (it is now regarded as a *Paranthropus*). The Leakeys had long known that Bed I contained very simple "Oldowan" tools consisting of rock "cores" from which sharp stone flakes had been bashed using hammerstones. The Oldowan material culture (the tools are often referred to as "Mode 1") clearly preceded anything then known from Europe; "Mode 2" handaxes comparable to those at the bottom of Mortillet's European sequence only appeared higher in the Olduvai geological section (though the Oldowan is now known in Europe, too). Leakey was deeply attached to the "Man the Toolmaker" concept that made the fabrication of implements the key criterion of humanness; and because he had accordingly expected Bed I to yield the fossil remains of a very early representative of the genus *Homo*, it was a bit disappointing to find a very robust australopith alongside those crude tools. For the time being, however, it was the only candidate for toolmaker.

But not for long. The "Zinj" discovery attracted funding, and efforts redoubled. Late the next year, very low in Bed I, fragmentary remains were found of

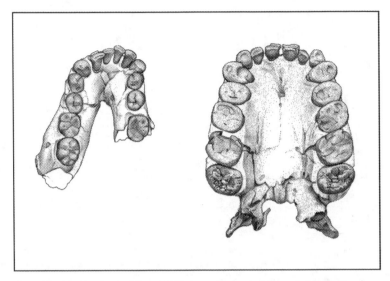

Figure 4.1   Mandibular dentition of OH7, type specimen of *Homo habilis* (left), compared with the upper dentition of the Olduvai Hominid 5 "Zinjanthropus" cranium (right) to give an idea of the radical difference in dental proportions. Not to exact scale.

a distinctive hominin that was much more lightly built than the massive Zinj. The molar teeth in the single available lower jaw (Figure 4.1, left) were nonetheless quite big compared to later hominins; and, frankly, if it had been discovered in South Africa nobody would have had any trouble classifying this specimen as a gracile australopith. But Leakey wasn't looking for an australopith – he was after the toolmaker, which in his book had to be a member of *Homo*. Still, the new jaw pretty clearly didn't look like anything previously attributed to the genus defined by *Homo sapiens*, and Leakey's first judgment in early 1961 was that the specimen had belonged to "a remote and truly primitive ancestor of *Homo*." How remote, he didn't know; but he was soon to find out. Later in 1961, two Berkeley geochronologists joined him in announcing the first ever potassium–argon date in paleoanthropology, which placed the base of Bed I at an astonishing 1.8 myr (Leakey had himself

informally guessed 600 kyr). This almost unimaginable extension of the hominin timeline shook paleoanthropology to its core.

Fast-forward to 1964. By that time, several other hominin fragments had been
found in Bed I and the overlying lower Bed II at Olduvai. These included some
hand and foot bones, and some cranial fragments that suggested a largish brain
volume of around 680 ml; Leakey concluded that all belonged to the same
hominin as the gracile jaw. In 1964 Leakey and the anatomists Phillip Tobias
and John Napier bit the bullet and published them together as representing
a new species of *Homo*, *Homo habilis* ("handy man," since it was
a toolmaker). This was an absolutely mind-boggling extension of the morphology of our genus, but Leakey and colleagues pointed to that apparent
expansion of the brain. And then, of course, there were the stone tools.
Those were what almost certainly clinched the deal for Leakey's co-
describers; and indeed, without the tools the attribution to *Homo* would
never have been made, no matter how much Leakey, a long-time critic of
the australopiths, wanted to see a truly ancient *Homo* in his backyard.

Predictably enough, this absurd extension of the genus *Homo* back into very
remote time and australopith-like morphologies provoked a great deal of grumbling among colleagues who were shy of using zoological names, let alone of
creating new species. Eventually, that grumbling was allayed by further developments in East Africa, although in the meantime Ralph von Koenigswald (of
Pithecanthropus fame) and Leakey's collaborator Phillip Tobias had got
together over their respective fossils, and concluded that similar successions
of "grades" of human evolution could be seen in both eastern Africa and eastern
Asia, finding that (slightly) bigger-toothed hominins had given way to (slightly)
smaller-toothed ones in both regions. Most importantly, though, their paper is
emblematic of the conflicted state of mid-twentieth-century paleoanthropology.
For although the anglophone South African Tobias's Synthesis-inspired perspective dominated their report, the profusion of poorly defined names they
trotted out reflects von Koenigswald's attachment to the old anatomical outlook
that still lingered in continental Europe.

In 1967 the expedition outfitter Richard Leakey, representing his ailing father, led
the Kenyan contingent of an international paleontological survey in southern
Ethiopia's Omo Basin. His group recovered two partial skulls: one fragmentary

but of modern appearance, and the other a fairly complete braincase of more archaic aspect. Both are now estimated to be over 200 myr old, but at the time dating was hugely uncertain. Wearying of being a junior partner in a large enterprise led by the American Clark Howell (who had designed the first truly multidisciplinary paleoanthropological enterprise, with geochronologists, taphonomists, stratigraphers, and so forth, in addition to its paleontologists), Richard borrowed the expedition helicopter and overflew deposits just to the south, around Lake Turkana (then known as Lake Rudolf) in his homeland of Kenya. On landing he immediately saw fossils eroding from the deposits, and the die was cast. He appealed to the National Geographic Society for funds, and in the next year he began surveying deposits to the east of the lake.

Immediately, the expedition hit paydirt, in the form of a cranium (given the exotic name of KNM-ER 406; Figure 4.2, upper right) that resembled the

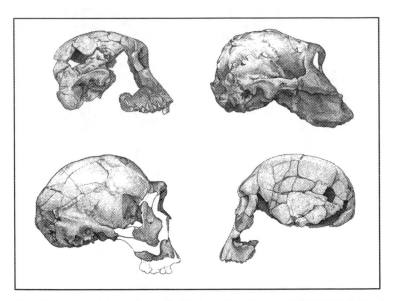

Figure 4.2   Four hominin crania from East Turkana, Kenya. Top row: KNM-ER 732 (left) and KNM-ER 406. Bottom row: KNM-ER 3733 (left) and KNM-ER 1470. Not to exact scale.

Olduvai "Zinj," although it had a much shallower face; and parts soon turned up of another, more lightly built, skull that was reported as a potential *Homo*. Also found were stone tools like those from Olduvai Bed I. These were associated with a volcanic tuff, known as the KBS, that was initially and erroneously K/Ar dated to 2.5 myr, but is actually half a million years younger. The situation thus appeared to be like that at Olduvai, with robust australo-piths and a tool-using *Homo* already distinct at a very early date. Just for the record, although he was not technically a paleoanthropologist, Richard had a true paleoanthropologist's disdain for systematics: He insisted that any gracile Turkana hominin fossil not be assigned to a species, but just to the indeterminate "*Homo* sp."

In subsequent years, the finds came thick and fast. In 1970, a small 1.7-myr-old partial cranium turned up that was dubbed ER 732 (Figure 4.2, upper left). All agreed that it was a female of the same robust australopith species as ER 406. As such, this specimen finally put an end to the "single-species hypoth-esis" that had held that the highly distinctive robust and gracile South African australopiths were males and females of a single species that was the progeni-tor of the later *Homo*. In 1971 another East Turkana locality called Ileret yielded a 1.5-myr-old lower jaw, with a modestly sized dentition, that vaguely reminded many of Asian *Homo erectus*. In 1975 Colin Groves and Vratislav Mazak (neither of them part of the Turkana team) gave this fossil its own species identity as *Homo ergaster* ("work man," for the tools). And in 1972, the team recovered the cranium, known as ER 1470 (Figure 4.2, lower right), that finally convinced many that *Homo habilis* was a real thing. Shattered and toothless, and found just beneath the KBS tuff, this skull proved on reconstruc-tion to have contained a brain of around 800 ml. Richard and his father hadn't agreed about much, but given its brain volume they concurred that ER 1470 belonged in *Homo*, proving that our genus had truly ancient African roots. As usual, Richard was reluctant to assign his specimen to a particular species of the genus, although he insisted on its erroneous early date until the bitter end. In truth, it is still hard to know what the poorly preserved ER 1470 represents; but for many observers its large brain volume appeared to validate *Homo habilis*, especially after the influential Clark Howell had identified another lightly built (though small-brained) Turkana cranium (ER 1813: 510 ml) as a female of the species.

Much more informative about early *Homo* were two crania recovered in East Turkana between 1974 and 1976. ER 3733 (Figure 4.2, lower left) is a pretty complete cranium with a brain volume of 850 ml that was initially thought to be about 1.9 myr old (a date since revised to 1.63 myr); and ER 3883 is a braincase with one preserved orbit that is of about the same age, and that had contained a brain of about 800 ml. Neither skull particularly closely resembles the other; and neither at all resembles the >0.7-myr-old Trinil skullcap from Java (Figure 3.2, left), with its shelf-like supraorbital region and sharply angled occiput, or even the slightly more rotund Beijing material (Figure 3.2, right). Nonetheless, in a first departure from the *Homo* sp. rule, and apparently in thrall again to brain volume, the Leakey team trumpeted the resemblances of these skulls to eastern Asian *Homo erectus*, the species to which they eventually assigned them. Thus was born the enduring myth that very early *Homo erectus* had existed in Africa, representing the beginning of a "stage" of human evolution that lay intermediate between the australopiths (or maybe *Homo habilis*) and *Homo sapiens*. Paleoanthropology had returned to the state in which Gustav Schwalbe had left it at the turn of the century.

The "early African *Homo erectus*" notion received a fillip in 1984 when a Leakey team, working at Nariokotome to the west of Lake Turkana, discovered the remarkably complete skeleton of an adolescent hominin who had died in a lakeside swamp some 1.6 myr ago (Figure 6.1). Showing the degree of skeletal maturity typical of a modern human 13-year-old, but already some five feet three inches tall and with a brain of 880 ml volume (that would, it's estimated, have reached over 900 ml at maturity), this individual was sufficiently developed to show that adults of his species had been very unlike any australopith. Taller, more slenderly built, and with limb proportions (longer legs, shorter arms) quite close to ours, the species to which the "Nariokotome Boy" had belonged was the earliest hominin known that had clearly committed itself to life out on the open savanna, away from the ancestral trees; and the Leakey group not only stressed its modern attributes, but emphasized its attribution to *Homo erectus* in a monograph published in 1993.

In 1995, a bit to the south of Nariokotome and in sediments about 2.5 myr old, the West Turkana group found the toothless cranium of a robust australopith with a protruding face. It is usually known for technical reasons as *Australopithecus* (or *Paranthropus*) *aethiopicus*, and it has been seen as the progenitor of the later robust lineages in both eastern and southern Africa.

Ethiopia and Tanzania: *Australopithecus afarensis* and *Ardipithecus ramidus*

While the Leakey group was making waves in Kenya, another spinoff from the Howell expedition was making equally dramatic discoveries in the Afar region of northeastern Ethiopia. Don Johanson, one of Clark Howell's graduate students, had accepted an invitation to join the French geologist Maurice Taieb in the latter's field area in the Afar region, which lies at the northern end of the great East African Rift Valley in which the Turkana and Olduvai sediments are also found. Taieb's promise of fossils galore eroding from what he thought were Plio-Pleistocene sediments was borne out, and the next year Johanson and the American geologist Jon Kalb joined him in a survey during which they homed in on the desert badlands at a place called Hadar, on the banks of the Awash River. During the 1973 field season they discovered the knee of a biped that they estimated had lived about 3 myr ago; and in 1974 they hit the real paydirt with Johanson's discovery of the fossil that is technically called NME (National Museum of Ethiopia) AL 288-1, but that became better known as "Lucy" (Figure 4.3). At the time, the tiny Lucy (who had stood not much over three feet tall) was the most complete skeleton of an australopith ever discovered; and although she lacked most of her skull, she was complete enough to provide an image of what the entire individual had been like in life, providing a poignant image of a young bipedal female who had died alone in the Ethiopian bush some 3.18 million years ago. As if this wasn't enough, the next year's fieldwork produced the remains of the "First Family," an amazing collection of over 200 fossil fragments that represented at least a dozen individuals who varied greatly in size, but who appeared to have perished together in a single dramatic event, maybe a flash flood. One mandible is seen in Figure 4.4 (left). So, who were they? Richard Leakey had stopped by early on for a visit, and had opined that, since a couple of lower jaws already discovered were clearly not those of robust australopiths, they must be "early *Homo*." Johanson picked up on this view in early descriptions of the Hadar material; but that was to change.

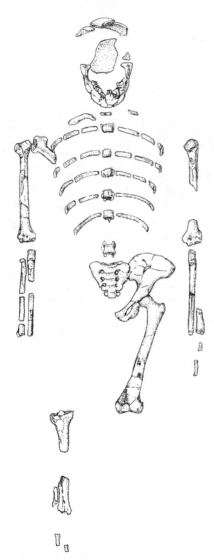

Figure 4.3   The skeleton from Hadar, Ethiopia that is officially known as NME AL 488-1, and more informally as "Lucy."

By the time the First Family was discovered, the political situation in Ethiopia had seriously deteriorated, and shortly thereafter fieldwork came to a halt for several years, though not before Mode 1 stone tools had shown up at a site called Gona that turned out to date from about 2.6 myr ago. And not before a group led by Jon Kalb had prospected younger deposits some distance upriver, in the Middle Awash area, and had found a partial cranium at a place called Bodo. Later dated to 600 kyr (almost exactly the age of the Mauer *Homo heidelbergensis* jaw from Germany with which it came to be classified), it reminded many of the Zambia skull (Figure 7.1, center) that Arthur Smith Woodward had assigned to *Homo rhodesiensis*, and its discoverers described it as "less archaic" than Asian *Homo erectus*. The Middle Awash eventually proved to have important fossil-bearing deposits spanning some 6 myr. But meanwhile, attention was turning to the Tanzanian site of Laetoli, to which Mary Leakey had returned following Louis's death in 1973. A hominin jaw fragment had been found there prewar, and between 1974 and 1982 Mary's team discovered some 30 more hominin fossils that ranged from single teeth to two partial lower jaws (one of them shown in Figure 4.4, right). The crown jewel, though, was the numerous footprint trails, some hominin, that had been made in wet volcanic ash about 3.6 myr ago. Here, finally, was direct evidence (conclusions from bony anatomy are necessarily inferential)

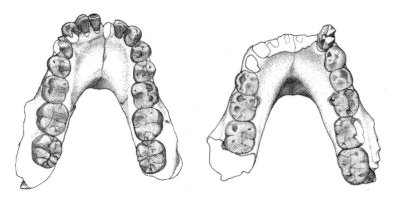

Figure 4.4 Two mandibles assigned to *Australopithecus afarensis*: AL 200-1a from Hadar, Ethiopia (left) and NMT-LH4 from Laetoli, Tanzania (right).

that hominins were walking erect at that remote time: The details of the prints have been debated, but nobody doubts that they were made by fully upright hominin bipeds.

Who had made the footprints? The first report on the associated hominin fossils was made by a team member called Tim White, who hewed to the Leakey party line and said nothing about what they were. But after White had brought casts of the Laetoli fossils to Cleveland, Ohio, where Johanson's team were studying the Afar materials, a different story emerged. There was a great deal of size variation at Hadar, so was one very variable hominin species involved, or two more typical ones? In 1978, after a drama that involved Mary Leakey's withdrawal from authorship and the trashing of an initial print run, Johanson and White (together with the French paleontologist Yves Coppens) went for the single-species idea, classifying the Ethiopian and Tanzanian fossils together in the same new species, which they called *Australopithecus afarensis*. Largely because of its great age, Johanson and White saw this hominin as the common progenitor of both the robust and gracile australopiths, and of *Homo*; and they said so explicitly in 1979. Not everyone concurred at the time, and doubts persist, although *A. afarensis* itself is undoubtedly a convenience that neatly ties up a lot of loose ends. Which is useful, if not necessarily illuminating, because in paleoanthropology we are dealing with a very closely knit group, within which lines are almost inevitably going to be tricky to draw.

The moratorium on Ethiopian fieldwork was not lifted until 1989, by which time Jon Kalb had been forced out of the country, his permit in the Middle Awash assumed by the Berkeley archaeologist Desmond Clark. An early discovery was of a handful of associated teeth and other fragments described in 1994 from a 4.4-myr-old site called Aramis. Clark's by-then University of California, Berkeley colleague Tim White and two colleagues first named them *Australopithecus ramidus*, but changed the moniker the next year to *Ardipithecus ramidus*, making their new form the only pre-*Australopithecus* hominin known. Nearby was found a skeleton (Figure 5.1) so fragile that it took many years to prepare and was described only in 2009. It showed that while "Ardi" had a tiny 350 ml brain, it also had a reduced canine complex, and a possible tendency to upright posture – although its foot had a notably divergent (grasping) great toe. The apparent time range of the genus was later increased by the discovery of some 5.2–5.8-myr-old fragments that were assigned to the new species *Ardipithecus kadabba*.

Much later in time, a Middle Awash topographical feature known as the Bouri Peninsula produced some 2.5-myr-old australopith remains, named *Australopithecus garhi*, along with mammal bones that bore the telltale "cutmarks" made by butchery with stone cutting tools. Here, the Berkeley team broadly hinted, was proof that it was not only members of *Homo* who had made stone tools. Higher in the Bouri section, a site called Daka produced a 1-myr-old braincase, with a volume of 995 ml, that was predictably described in 2002 as a *Homo erectus* (although that assignment was later soundly refuted by Italian researchers affiliated to the group that had found a cranium of similar age and volume, but rather different aspect, not far away at the Eritrean site of Buia). And at the top of the Bouri sediment pile, a place called Herto yielded some crania that the team described as the "probable immediate ancestor[s] of anatomically modern humans." Naming subspecies is generally unwise when you are dealing with fossils, but the Herto skulls (Figure 8.3) were nonetheless given their own subspecies identity, as *Homo sapiens idaltu*. A particularly remarkable common denominator among these discoveries, scattered though almost 6 myr in time, was that each one was claimed to lie more or less directly in the ancestral line to *Homo sapiens*.

At Hadar more discoveries were also being made. A palate dated to 2.3 myr, from sediments containing Mode 1 tools, was assigned to "early *Homo*," although not too many eyebrows would have been raised had it been described as a late *Australopithecus afarensis*. Two broken but fairly complete skulls of that species were found at the 3 myr level: a larger male with a brain volume of 550 ml, and a smaller female. And right across the Awash River, in an area known as Dikika, a team led by the Ethiopian paleoanthropologist Zeray Alemseged later discovered the quasi-complete skeleton of an infant who had died some 3.3 myr ago at the age of three. In 3.4-myr-old sediments nearby, the Alemseged group also discovered cut-marked bones that suggested the mammals concerned had been butchered using sharp stone flakes – long before the earliest Mode 1 tools appeared, at about 2.6 myr ago. The only even vaguely comparable finding, published in 2015, is of knapped flakes some 3.3 myr old at the Lomekwi 3 site at West Turkana. These are oddly large, nothing at all like the Oldowan; and although currently an outlier, they tantalizingly suggest that the latter might not have been quite the beginning of the stone tool story.

Chad, Kenya, and Ethiopia: *Sahelanthropus*, *Orrorin*, and *Kenyanthropus*

Just to the south of Lake Turkana, Richard Leakey's wife, Meave, had been carrying out her own investigations near a place called Kanapoi, where a hominin elbow had been found back in the 1960s. In 1995, Meave Leakey and collaborators described some hominin remains from Kanapoi and the nearby site of Allia Bay as *Australopithecus anamensis*. Dated to between 4.4 and 3.9 myr ago, this was the earliest and most primitive species of its genus; but it had unquestionably been a biped, as demonstrated by the structure of a preserved ankle joint. Not to be outdone, in 2006 the Middle Awash group claimed that some fragments from the 4.1–4.2 myr site of Assa Issie placed *A. anamensis* in the middle of a series that transformed gradually from *Ardipithecus ramidus* to *Au. afarensis*. Even the rival Hadar scientists got in on the act, claiming that a single lineage had evolved from the Kanapoi form, via the later Allia Bay fossils, to those from Laetoli, and finally to Hadar *Au. afarensis*. Eventually, those gradualist reveries were to be rudely trashed by the Ethiopian paleoanthropologist Yohannes Haile-Selassie. Haile-Selassie, a former associate of Tim White, had gone out on his own in 2004 to explore the Woranso-Mille region to the east of Hadar. In 2005 he reported discovering the partial skeleton of a large *Australopithecus*, dating from 3.6 myr ago; and in 2015 his group ascribed some upper and lower jaws to a 3.3–3.5-myr-old new species they called *Au. deyiremeda*. Finally, in 2019 they announced having also found at Woranso-Mille the first, 3.8-myr-old, cranium of *Au. anamensis* (Figure 4.5, left). This specimen not only differed more than expected from its counterpart in *Au. afarensis*, but had overlapped with it in time, demonstrating that, instead of merging insensibly, the two *Australopithecus* lineages had coexisted as distinct entities for at least 100 kyr.

In the 1990s the idea had caught on that the ER 1470 skull (Figure 4.2, lower right) might not be *Homo habilis* after all, and thus needed its own species name (which the intervention of a Russian anthropologist meant had to be

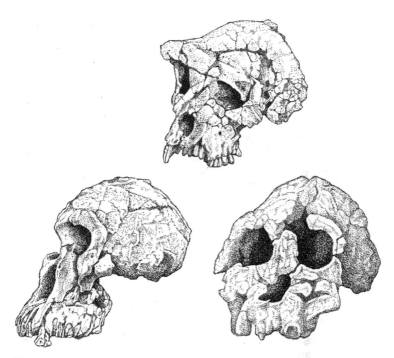

Figure 4.5   Left: Cranium (NME-MRD-VP-1/1) assigned to *Australopithecus anamensis*, from Woranso-Mille, Ethiopia. Center: Type cranium (TM 266-01-060-1) of *Sahelanthropus tchadensis*, from Toros-Menalla, Chad. Right: *Kenyanthropus platyops* type cranium KNM-WT 40000 from West Turkana, Kenya. Not to scale.

rudolfensis). Other specimens subsequently also accreted to this species, including a 2.5-myr-old lower jaw found in Malawi in 1992 and a 1.8-myr-old palate found at Olduvai in 1995. Then, in 1999, Meave Leakey's group found a very crushed and shattered 3.5-myr-old hominin skull (WT 40000) at a West Turkana site (Figure 4.5, right). So distinctive was it, that they found it required its own genus as well as species. They chose the name *Kenyanthropus platyops* (flat-faced man of Kenya) to reflect its most obvious morphological attribute, which it happened to share with the favored reconstruction of ER 1470. They consequently proposed that both lay in the same *Kenyanthropus* lineage, separate from the australopiths, and that the earlier *K. platyops* had given rise to the later *K. rudolfensis*. And there, despite some strenuous initial objections, the matter still rests.

Meanwhile, other entrants were intruding on *Ardipithecus* in the "earliest hominin" stakes. In 2000 some broken femoral shafts and pieces of jaw were found in 6-myr-old deposits near Lake Baringo, in northern Kenya. In the following year they were named *Orrorin* ("original man") *tugenensis* by Martin Pickford and Brigitte Senut, of the Collège de France. With their bluntish canines, squarish molar teeth, and suggestive femoral fragments, these fossils were plausibly if not definitively the early hominids they were claimed to be. But the French researchers went on to sideline *Ardipithecus* to the status of ancestral chimpanzee, and to argue that an early split in the hominin lineage had led to *Orrorin* and ultimately *Homo*, on the one hand, and to an australopith dead-end on the other. That interpretation failed to receive much support, and shortly a more dramatic claimant for earliest hominin came on the scene. This was *Sahelanthropus tchadensis*, a crushed cranium recovered from sediments probably close to 7 myr old in the central-western African country of Chad. A few years earlier, Chad had produced a rather enigmatic 3.6-myr-old australopith jaw fragment that had been called *Australopithecus bahrelghazali*. Named in 2002, *Sahelanthropus* was virtually reconstructed in 2005 (Figure 4.5, center) and proved to have had a brain of only around 350 ml. It also had a protruding face that contained reduced (if pointy) canine teeth, and rather nondescript molars which could easily have been hominin. Most tellingly, the foramen magnum was positioned beneath the skull, which had therefore been balanced atop the vertical spine of an upright biped. By early in the new millennium, then, three different African candidates in the 5–7-myr range (*Sahelanthropus*, *Orrorin*, and *Ar. ramidus*) were already vying for the title of "earliest hominin," and there was quite compelling evidence that, in some way, hominins were up on two feet by around seven million years ago.

Exodus from Africa: *Homo georgicus*

As late as the end of the 1980s it appeared that hominins had been confined to Africa until about a million years ago, though there were a few apparently anomalous earlier dates in Eurasia for what might have been hominin sites. Then came an amazing discovery at Dmanisi, a ruined medieval town in the Republic of Georgia, in the southern Caucasus between the Black and Caspian Seas. In 1991, medieval archaeologists discovered fossils poking out of the walls of storage pits dug by the long-vanished Dmanisi townsfolk. The sediments into which the pits were excavated rest on a lava flow now dated to 1.8 myr ago, and over the past quarter-century they have produced a huge fossil fauna and numerous Mode 1 tools, in addition to five hominin crania, four lower jaws, and three postcranial skeletons. The first hominin found was a mandible attributed in 1995 to "archaic African *Homo erectus*," a rather ambiguous designation that was nonetheless generally accepted without demur. Two crania with modest cranial volumes of 650 and 789 ml followed in 2000, and then an astonishing second lower jaw in 2001. This was radically unlike the first mandible: It was much larger and more heavily built, and had far more heavily worn teeth.

In 2006 the dig director David Lordkipanidze joined with the French paleoanthropologist Marie-Antoinette de Lumley to classify this remarkable specimen in the new species *Homo georgicus*. Shortly thereafter, however, a 600 ml-volume skull (Figure 4.6, right) was found that reminded the Dmanisi group of some East Turkana crania, and the entire assemblage was shifted back to *Homo erectus*, as the "most primitive individuals so far attributed" to that species. The 2002 discovery of the cranium and mandible of an aged male (625 ml), who had survived to a considerable age despite possessing only a single tooth, did not lead to any taxonomic rethinking, but a review in 2006 affirmed the view that, despite their morphological disparities, all the Dmanisi hominins belonged to a single species. According to a report on the postcranial bones that was published in 2007, that species was bipedal but diminutive, barely five feet tall; and though its limb proportions were relatively modern (but with "primitive features"), its foot structure suggested a gait unlike our own.

The Dmanisi single-species judgment came despite the discovery, in the previous year, of the cranium that matched the large lower jaw (Figure 4.6, left). This cranium turned out not only to be completely unlike all the other crania from the site, but vastly different from any other hominin yet discovered. It has the small braincase (525 ml) and strongly protruding face of a gracile australopith, but it is very different in its anatomical details. Yet if it

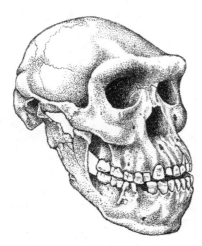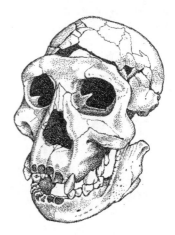

Figure 4.6 Two skulls from Dmanisi, Republic of Georgia. Left, D4500/2600 (Skull 5); right, D2700/2735. The individual on the left is aged; the one on the right is subadult. Not to scale.

isn't an australopith, it's not like any accepted member of *Homo*, either. Perhaps it is something else? Well, that is something that a science of paleoanthropology still in thrall to Ernst Mayr isn't yet ready to consider; the only acceptable algorithm nowadays seems to be that "if it isn't an australopith, then it must be *Homo*." Or vice-versa. And in the case of Dmanisi Skull 5, as the big specimen is known, the team showed the ultimate equivocation: In its formal description of the specimen, published in 2013, they allocated it to *Homo erectus ergaster georgicus*, a taxonomically illegal designation that allowed them to cover all thinkable possibilities.

All of this was taking place against the background of a 1992 review of the genus *Homo* by the former Turkana team member and paleoanthropologist Bernard Wood, as updated with his student Mark Collard in 1999. By the 1990s, the morphological boundaries of the genus defined by *Homo sapiens* had been expanding for several decades through the steady accretion of specimens with new features; and to anyone's eyes but those of a paleoanthropologist, it was clearly bursting at the seams. Remarkably, even as late as the turn of the century Wood and Collard still felt obliged to begin their analysis by rejecting the "Man the Toolmaker" concept, thereby excluding the Dmanisi stone tools from relevance in this context. They then correctly pointed out that genera should be monophyletic (all members descended from the same common ancestor), although they immediately muddied the waters by objecting that a monophyletic group might nonetheless contain species that were differently "adapted." They consequently proposed restricting genera to forms occupying "a single adaptive zone," whatever that might mean. Still, this was a criterion of sorts; and in applying it to *Homo*, Wood and Collard found that it excluded the fossils that had been allocated to *Homo habilis* and *Homo rudolfensis*. This left *Homo* just with species that had both body skeletons and jaws and teeth of broadly modern proportions. The East African "*erectus*" fossils (for which many were by now using the name *Homo ergaster*) would be in; but all the wildly differing Dmanisi hominins – had they not all come from the same site, there is no way that all would have been classified in the same species – would be out. Just for the record, cranially *Homo ergaster* and the defining species *Homo sapiens* differ a great deal more than you usually see within the same mammalian genus; but Wood and Collard's new formulation nonetheless served to tidy up the genus *Homo* very nicely (although fending off the rejects into *Australopithecus* made the latter a lot messier). But almost inevitably, things would soon start to get complicated again.

The "Hobbit" and Other Surprises: *Homo floresiensis* and *Homo naledi*

Excavations in 2003–2004 produced a truly stunning discovery at the Liang Bua cave in the Indonesian island of Flores. Levels in the cave floor now dated to between 60 and 100 kyr ago yielded numerous hominin fossils, including a partial skeleton known as LB1. Now thought to have been female, LB1 was fully adult but had stood only about three feet six inches tall, weighing maybe 77 pounds. Her cranial vault had contained a brain of only 380 ml, and her diminutive dentition is set in a distinctive, short, and delicately built face (Figure 4.7, left). Her body proportions are equally surprising: her rather short legs are matched with astonishingly long and flat feet; her pelvis flares noticeably, a bit like an australopith's; and she appears to have held her shoulders hunched forward. A second lower jaw and other fossils are much like their counterparts in LB1, showing that she is no freak; and associated stone tools and animal bones suggest that these "hobbits" who had lived in Liang Bua from about 190 to 50 kyr ago had been successful hunters.

What was this strange creature from Flores? From the beginning, there were those who thought the hominin remains pathological, the result of any one of a whole variety of diseases. Candidate conditions have, however, been systematically eliminated by careful study. It's additionally very unlikely that all members of a population with a history of many tens of thousands of years of occupation at Liang Bua should have had the same pathology; and at the nearby site of Mata Menge quite similar (but 700-kyr-old) fossils have also been found in association with stone tools. The Flores hominin is evidently a genuine biological entity, leaving two possibilities: Either LB1 and her like were descended from a very small ancestor, or they were "dwarfed" from a larger one, as many mammals stranded on islands become. In the latter case, the obvious ancestor would be *Homo erectus*, known from a record in nearby Java that had greatly expanded since von Koenigswald's time. But unlike Java,

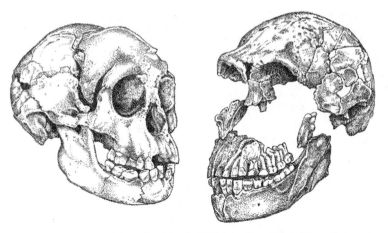

Figure 4.7   The crania of *Homo floresiensis* (LB1) from Liang Bua in Flores, Indonesia (left), and *Homo naledi* (LES1) from the Rising Star cave complex in South Africa (right). Not to scale.

Flores had been isolated by a sea barrier from the Asian mainland, and from Java itself, even during the lowest sea-level stands of the Pleistocene. And I am at a loss to discover any specifically *Homo erectus* features in the Flores form that would suggest such a relationship, even though computer modeling suggests that, in principle, small body size might have been achieved in a relatively short time. It's much more likely, then, that the Flores hominin was descended (even possibly dwarfed) from a much more morphologically primitive ancestor whose lineage must have left its natal continent of Africa at a remarkably early date. Its descendant's residence in Flores seems to have been eventually ended by modern humans, who were building hearths in Liang Bua by 41 kyr ago.

In 2004 the Liang Bua team published their new find in the journal *Nature*, as *Homo floresiensis*. Legend has it that they wanted to call it *Australopithecus floresiensis*, but reviewers insisted on the change to *Homo*. Whether that is true or not, there are considerable objections either way, and neither designation is satisfactory. We are, of course, seeing here yet another application of the *Australopithecus*/*Homo* dichotomy that continues to prevent us from properly representing hominin diversity in the nomenclature we use. An addition to that past hominin diversity in insular southeast Asia came in 2019, from the Callao cave in the northern Philippines. There, researchers reported finding a handful of very small teeth and some (adult) bones of a hominin that had lived there between 67 and 50 kyr ago. One foot bone was sufficiently strongly curved to invite comparison with *Australopithecus*, but the limited ensemble was published as *Homo luzonensis*. A window is opening into what may prove to be an entire radiation of small-bodied and small-brained Pleistocene hominins in an area where the only possible dispersal was by sea.

In 2013 news broke of an astonishing discovery in South Africa, very close to the classic australopith sites of Sterkfontein and Swartkrans. Deep within a system of limestone caves known as Rising Star, spelunkers had located an almost inaccessible underground chamber, the floor of which appeared to be littered with hominin fossils. Immediately the paleoanthropologist Lee Berger (who had previously discovered, nearby, fossils of a 2-myr-old australopith species that he had named *Australopithecus sediba*) advertised for slender volunteers (at one point inside the cave they had to squeeze through a reported eight-inch gap), who soon began retrieving fossils by the hundreds. By late 2014 over 1,500 specimens, representing at least 15 individuals and virtually all of the skeleton, had been recovered from the main Dinaledi Chamber; and soon thereafter another 130 fragments from three more individuals had been retrieved from the Lesedi Chamber, part of the same cave system but separately accessed. All the fossils appeared to represent the same kind of hominin. An international research group was assembled, and in 2015 the Dinaledi assemblage was astonishingly quickly published, as the new species *Homo naledi*.

The newly described hominin had been an upright biped with a small body (standing a little under five feet tall) and a small brain (cranial volumes between about 465 and 560 ml). It was reported to have a rather australopith-like upper body, pelvis, and upper leg, in conjunction with more human-like hands (albeit with rather curved fingers) and feet. Some features of the upper limb suggest arboreal capabilities. The cranial proportions of *Homo naledi* most closely resemble those of gracile australopiths, with a strongly jutting face hafted in front of a small braincase (Figure 4.7, right), but the dentition reportedly "compares most favorably to early *Homo*." This made up a curious combination of features that only superficially invited comparison with the Flores hominin, and that made it clear that the Rising Star hominin's assignment to *Homo* was once again a diagnosis of exclusion: Clearly this was no australopith, so *Homo* it had to be. At the beginning its age was not known, but its tiny brain had suggested to most that it was quite ancient, probably having lived well over 1.5 myr ago. So, imagine the amazement that erupted in 2017 on the news that a combination of electron spin resonance (ESR) on teeth, uranium–thorium on flowstone, and paleomagnetic dating had come in with a date range for the Dinaledi fossils of 236–335 kyr!

Somehow, a hominin of very archaic appearance and extremely limited brain size had contrived to survive almost up to the emergence of our own species, not on a remote island but on the great continent of Africa, where it would all along have been in competition with several larger-bodied species of the genus *Homo*. Sadly, the Rising Star sites provided no archaeological context that might have helped explain this long survival, although the team eventually decided that the only way the bones could have got to where they were found was via deliberate disposal of the bodies. For one thing, there are no animal bite-marks on them, ruling out carnivore or scavenger activity; and for another (and very unusually for a South African site), the assemblage is made up exclusively of hominins. Not everyone agrees with the disposal interpretation, and although the lack of evidence for water activity in the cave may raise its likelihood somewhat, the researchers have so far steadfastly declined to speculate about the wider implications of such a practice.

Atapuerca and *Homo heidelbergensis*

The only other place in the world that can claim anything like Rising Star's paleoanthropological richness is the site known as the Sima de los Huesos (Pit of the Bones) in northern Spain's Atapuerca Massif. An abandoned nineteenth-century railway trench dug though the limestone massif inadvertently exposed a whole series of underground cavities containing ancient bones, and these were explored by paleoanthropologists beginning in the late 1980s. Among them was the Gran Dolina site, which yielded both Mode 1 tools and the 0.8-myr-old fossil fragments that provided the basis for the new species *Homo antecessor* in 1997. The Atapuerca team proposed that their new fossil might lie close to the common ancestry of Neanderthals and *Homo*, a conclusion that appears reinforced by a 2020 comparative study of proteins extracted from isolated teeth. They also suggested that the fragmentation of the *H. antecessor* remains was due to butchery for the purposes of cannibalism, which they claimed was not an unusual subsistence strategy among later Pleistocene European hominins.

The railway trench also exposed such remarkable sites as the Sima del Elefante that produced the oldest (1.2 myr) clear evidence of hominin occupation of Europe, both in the form of Mode 1 tools and of a fragment of lower jaw that the team suggested might represent an early *H. antecessor*. But the undisputed gem of Atapuerca is the Sima de los Huesos. This is an accumulation of fossil bones found in a small cavity at the bottom of a narrow, vertical 13-meter shaft that opens deep within a large cave. From this cramped space, excavators exhumed thousands of fragments that represented the remains of at least 28 hominin individuals who were eventually dated to around 430 kyr ago. The skull of one of them is shown in Figure 7.4 (left). There were a few carnivore bones in the deposit (no herbivores); but the fossils were overwhelmingly hominin, and the excavators, rejecting natural processes of accumulation, decided that the only convincing explanation for that pile of broken bodies was that they had been thrown in (already dead) by their fellows. Only one artifact was found in the Pit, a singularly beautiful handaxe that was interpreted as a funerary offering. Not everyone agrees, and the matter remains debated.

As to the hominins themselves, they were stocky (males averaging five feet seven inches tall, and females five feet two) and robustly built, with cranial vaults averaging 1230 ml in volume. They share with the Neanderthals various features of the face and dentition, but not of the braincase; and the obvious conclusion is that the Sima people represented a distinctive population that was somehow antecedent to the bigger-brained Neanderthals. Unfortunately, however, the Atapuerca team saw fit to allocate their fossils to *Homo heidelbergensis*. As you'll recall, this is the species defined by the Mauer jaw; and over the years it had come to contain a variety of fossils in the 600 to 200 kyr range (and with similar brain sizes to those of the Sima people) that included the Bodo and Kabwe (Rhodesian: Figure 7.1, center) skulls from Africa, a couple of skulls from China (Figure 7.1, right), a well-preserved cranium from Petralona in Greece (Figure 7.1, left), and both cranial and postcranial fossils from Tautavel in France. The Tautavel assemblage (initially described as "European *Homo erectus*") includes both a well-preserved face that has typical *H. heidelbergensis* features, and a mandible that has enough in common with the Mauer jaw to place both in the same species. *Homo heidelbergensis* as thus constituted has often been mooted as a potential ancestor for both modern humans and Neanderthals; and while its facial anatomy appears a bit too derived for this role, this species is certainly the first well-established cosmopolitan hominin, known from all major areas of the Old World. What it clearly is *not*, however, is conspecific with the Sima hominin, which requires its own species designation within the Neanderthal clade. The Sima researchers privately admit this, but they are reluctant to propose a new name for their fossils because it's possible they belong to *Homo steinheimensis*, the name given to a rather distorted cranium found in Germany in 1933 (Figure 7.4, right). Still, nomenclature aside, what the Sima fossils most importantly do is to give the Neanderthal clade a presence in Europe (distinct from *H. heidelbergensis*) that goes back to at least 430 kyr ago.

Homo neanderthalensis, Early *Homo sapiens*, and Genomics

Our knowledge of the Neanderthals themselves increased by leaps and bounds as more sites were discovered in the postwar years, during which improvements in dating and field techniques took their fossil record back to around 200 kyr ago. The same period also saw extreme swings in how the Neanderthals were viewed. In 1964 Loring Brace, a paleoanthropologist at the University of Michigan, launched a sweeping attack on all who would exclude the Neanderthals from direct human ancestry, and the cry was soon taken up by his colleague Milford Wolpoff, one of the architects of the "Multiregional Evolution" hypothesis which basically resuscitated Franz Weidenreich's idea that the modern geographic varieties of humankind had very deep roots, evolving in parallel while exchanging enough genes to maintain the integrity of the species. This could not be done by making the Neanderthals directly ancestral to modern humans, because by now their abrupt replacement in Europe by invading *Homo sapiens* was plainly documented; instead, it was done by subsuming the Neanderthals into *Homo sapiens* despite their manifold morphological differences between the two. Eventually, the Multiregional people realized that the logic of their scheme dictated doing the same for virtually everything that had lived after "early *Homo*." This was a final *reductio ad absurdum* that made some paleoanthropologists listen more closely to the proponents of the nascent "Out of Africa" scenario, which held that *Homo sapiens* had evolved in Africa and later spread out of the continent to compete with and replace the hominins already resident in other areas of the Old World.

As far as *Homo neanderthalensis* was concerned, however, by far the most revelatory development of recent decades has come from genomics (see Chapter 2). The then-nascent techniques of genomics had been applied to human evolution as early as 1975, when Allan Wilson of the University of California, Berkeley and his student Mary-Claire King had presciently shown that differences between chimpanzees and humans in protein-coding genes were insufficient by themselves to explain the morphological differences between them – and that those differences must thus have been due to differences in gene activity, rather than structure. By 1987, Wilson and his students Rebecca Cann and Mark Stoneking had also compared the mtDNAs of 147 people from around the world, concluding that the species *Homo sapiens* had arisen about 200 kyr ago in Africa – something that was substantiated from fossil evidence a couple of decades later.

For decades, genomic techniques could be applied only to living organisms such as *Homo sapiens*. But in 1997 it was announced that fragments of mtDNA had been extracted from Neanderthal fossils in the Munich laboratory of Svante Pääbo, founder of the rapidly expanding field of hominin paleogenomics. These samples not only fell outside the range of variation seen in a geographic array of modern humans, but were equidistant from all, reinforcing the identity of Neanderthals as a discrete species. The plot thickened significantly in 2010, when the Pääbo group, by then based in Leipzig, published the first Neanderthal nuclear genome. This turned out to be extraordinarily similar structurally to that of *Homo sapiens*, suggesting that King and Wilson had been right, and that regulation of gene activity was responsible for many of the observed phenotypic differences. The researchers made an initial calculation that the Neanderthal and modern lineages had parted ways between 300 and 700 kyr ago. Time estimates for this event have since fluctuated, but at its more distant end the original one is compatible with what we might infer from the fossil record.

More surprising was the finding of specific similarities between Neanderthal nuclear DNA, on the one hand, and that of modern human populations outside Africa, on the other. These commonalities were interpreted as evidence of hybridization between the resident Eurasian Neanderthals and the ultimately African *Homo sapiens* who began streaming into their western Asian homeland at an estimated 47–65 kyr ago; and they were said to be reflected among modern Europeans in a 2–4-percent possession of "Neanderthal DNA" (a figure since reduced to 1.5–2.1 percent).

After this, things moved quickly. In 2010 the Pääbo team announced that an mtDNA genome extracted from an undiagnostic finger bone found at southern Siberia's Denisova Cave was that of a distinctive hominin, related to the Neanderthals. It has yet to be given a formal species name. The same "Denisovan" specimen, now dated to around 60 kyr, also produced a nuclear genome that was published in 2013. This confirmed that the

Denisovans' closest relative was *Homo neanderthalensis*; and it also suggested, very approximately, that the two hominid lineages had split around 300 kyr ago and had shared a common ancestor with modern humans around 700 kyr ago. Other fragmentary specimens from Denisova that carry the characteristic Denisovan DNA signature are older than the finger bone, up to about 200 kyr; and a rather nondescript partial mandible recently reported from a Chinese site high on the Himalayan Plateau is more than 160 kyr old. Poorly as they are known, then, the shadowy Denisovans were evidently widespread in Eurasia in their day. And they certainly made an impact: some 7–8 percent of their DNA is shared with modern Papuans, suggesting substantial episodes of interbreeding not only with Neanderthals but also with early modern humans who were presumably heading east. And, in some way, they evidently also shared their eponymous cave with Neanderthals between around 200 and 100 kyr ago: Both species left their traces there, and one fossil evidently had a Denisovan father and a Neanderthal mother! Interestingly, a 430-kyr-old bone fragment from Spain's Sima de los Huesos showed not only an mtDNA relationship with Neanderthals, but an even closer one with Denisovans (though a later analysis of nuclear DNA suggested otherwise). Such observations naturally started traditional paleoanthropologists wondering how much of the accepted Neanderthal fossil record might in fact be Denisovan: We still have no good idea of what these hominin phantoms looked like. And, just as intriguingly, the molecular researchers found DNA evidence of interbreeding between Denisovans and an additional "ghost" lineage, which might or might not be known from fossils.

As for the Neanderthals themselves, their DNA evidence has continued accumulating, and by now has even been retrieved from cave sediments in which there are no fossils (feces contain DNA). Several genomes are also known from early European *Homo sapiens* that show stronger Neanderthal signatures than are typical nowadays. Modern humans emerged as a distinctive anatomical entity in Africa over 200 kyr ago, and evidently left their natal continent and entered Eurasia on several different occasions after about 80 kyr ago, interbreeding with Neanderthals and Denisovans as they went. Interestingly, some 45-kyr-old early moderns from Bacho Kiro Cave in Romania not only had 3.0–3.8 percent Neanderthal DNA (apparently from only six generations back) but were also distantly related to a 40-kyr-old individual excavated at the

Tianyuan cave in China. They had evidently belonged to a modern lineage that went extinct in Europe, but that had continued farther east where it flourished until about 32 kyr ago when it vanished there as well. This pattern of migration, followed eventually by local extinction, seems to have been typical in the human past, repeated many times in many places. In Europe (as in eastern Asia), the peak of the last Ice Age seems to have ultimately had a purging effect, with widespread population replacement after the ice caps had retreated; but, oddly enough in this perspective, the height of the last glacial period in Europe saw the emergence of the Magdalenian culture and the largest outpouring of ancient art and creative expression yet documented, clearly the product of a prosperous society that was replaced by more impoverished ones as the climate warmed. A very complex history has evidently yet to be fully unraveled.

In 2021 an international group led by the Washington University neuropsychologist Robert Cloninger took a novel approach to interpreting the newly available nuclear DNA data on Neanderthals. They compared them not only to the nuclear genome of modern humans, but to that of chimpanzees as well. Previously, the group had identified 972 genes that regulate the three major component systems of modern human personality: emotional reactivity, self-control, and self-awareness. They discovered that Neanderthals possessed almost the same genes for emotional reactivity as chimpanzees, and that the extinct hominins were intermediate between chimpanzees and modern humans in the numbers of genes associated with self-control and self-awareness. They also found that 95 percent of the 267 genes (of the larger set) that are seen only in modern humans are regulatory, rather than protein-coding, and concluded that they are present in us because of strong selection for the uniquely human aspects of prosociality (basically, concern for others). These genes are also typically highly expressed in brain regions involved in self-awareness and creativity, all of which suggests that Neanderthals were cognitively very different from us – a finding that makes eminent sense in terms of the very distinctive archaeological records bequeathed us by Neanderthals and early behaviorally modern *Homo sapiens* (see Chapter 8).

It is important to note at this point that interbreeding between the Eurasian *Homo neanderthalensis* and the ultimately African *Homo sapiens*, although by now pretty solidly documented, does not greatly affect our view of the two species as differentiated entities. As noted in Chapter 1, species are reproductively leaky vessels, and some interbreeding is to be expected between very close relatives should the opportunity arise. Culturally, cognitively, and physically the Neanderthals were clearly very different from us; and we will see that evidence for potential cultural interchange is both limited and contested. Most significant in this context is that Neanderthals became extinct as a distinctive physical (and as far as we can tell cognitive) entity, while *Homo sapiens* went on to become the creature familiar today without any notable change, apart maybe from a minor reduction in brain size. True, there was some minor interspecies gene transfer: One legacy of the Denisovans was, for example, a gene that helped the ancestors of modern Tibetans colonize the extreme high-altitude habitat in which their descendants still live. And the Neanderthals have been credited and blamed for modern human alleles that are both protective against the COVID-19 disease, and that increase vulnerability to it. But in most important respects, *Homo sapiens* continued on its evolutionary trajectory essentially undisturbed. Indeed, the rather vestigial nature of the Neanderthal genetic contribution lingering in modern Eurasian populations seems to be due to active selection against "Neanderthal" genes since the extinction of the latter; and although a 2021 study somewhat surprisingly discovered that Africans on average have a detectable (0.3 percent) "Neanderthal" contribution to their genomes, this was found to be most plausibly due to back-migration of Eurasian populations into Africa.

The take-home message here is very similar to the overall one you will have derived from the previous two chapters, namely that the human story is much messier, and significantly less linear, than the one that was predicted by the Modern Evolutionary Synthesis that still so profoundly influences the paleoanthropological mindset today. There were many more actors in the human evolutionary play than we once believed, and we are still struggling to sort out the consequent complexities.

Table 4.1 summarizes the hominin species discussed in this chapter.

Original Name	Current Name	Named By	Date	Where Found	Age
Zinjanthropus boisei	P. boisei	L. Leakey	1959	Tanzania	1.8 myr
Homo habilis	H. habilis	L. Leakey +	1964	Tanzania	1.8 myr
Homo ergaster	H. ergaster	C. Groves +	1975	Kenya	1.5 myr
Homo heidelbergensis	H. heidelbergensis	O. Schoetensack	1908	Germany	600 kyr
Homo rhodesiensis	H. heidelbergensis	A. Woodward	1921	Malawi	~300 kyr
Australopithecus afarensis	A. afarensis	D. Johanson +	1978	Ethiopia/ Tanzania	3.4 myr
Australopithecus ramidus	Ar. ramidus	T. White +	1994	Ethiopia	4.4 myr
Ardipithecus kadabba	Ar. kadabba	Y. H-Selassie +	2004	Ethiopia	5.2 myr
Australopithecus garhi	A. garhi	B. Asfaw +	1999	Ethiopia	2.6 myr
Australopithecus anamensis	A. anamensis	M. Leakey +	1995	Kenya	4.2 myr
Australopithecus deyiremeda	A. deyiremeda	Y. H-Selassie +	2015	Ethiopia	3.4 myr
Kenyanthropus platyops	K. platyops	M. Leakey +	2001	Kenya	3.5 myr
Pithecanthropus rudolfensis	K. rudolfensis	V. Alexeev	1986	Kenya	1.9 myr
Orrorin tugenensis	O. tugenensis	B. Senut +	2001	Kenya	6.0 myr
Australopithecus bahrelghazali	A. bahrelghazali	M. Brunet +	1996	Chad	<3.5 myr
Sahelanthropus tchadensis	S. tchadensis	M. Brunet +	2001	Chad	~7.0 myr
Homo georgicus	H. georgicus	M. Lumley +	2006	Rep. Georgia	1.8 myr
Homo floresiensis	"H." floresiensis	P. Brown +	2004	Flores, Indonesia	60 kyr
Homo luzonensis	"H." luzonensis	F. Detroit +	2019	Luzon, Philippines	67 kyr
Australopithecus sediba	A. sediba	L. Berger +	2010	South Africa	1.98 myr

Original Name	Current Name	Named By	Date	Where Found	Age
Homo naledi	*"H." naledi*	L. Berger +	2015	South Africa	~300 kyr
Homo antecessor	*H. antecessor*	J. B. Castro +	1997	Spain	780 kyr
Homo steinheimensis	*H. steinheimensis*	F. Berckhemer	1936	Germany	~300 kyr

kyr, thousand years; myr, million years; A., Australopithecus; Ar., Ardipithecus; K, Kenyanthropus; O., Orrorin; P., Paranthropus; S., Sahelanthropus.

Table 4.1 Summary of the principal hominin species discussed in this chapter (by order of mention) with the original name, by whom named ("+" indicates multiple authors, first only given), and the name by which the species is known currently (by this author). Date is that of original publication, and age and locality are those of the type specimen.

5 Early Bipeds

Why Bipedality?

Seven million years ago the continent of Africa, actively bulging upward along the north–south line of the volcanically active Great Rift Valley, was also experiencing climatic drying and increased seasonality of rainfall due to a general oceanic cooling. Particularly to the east of the Rift, the formerly ubiquitous forests were giving way to woodlands and bushlands, and even to some early grasslands, stressing the populations of large-bodied, tailless, and mainly fruit-eating apes that the Miocene forests of both Africa and Eurasia had harbored in profusion. But the stress of change also brought with it opportunity, in the form of the very different range of potential food resources offered by the expansion of more open environments. And while modern apes living partially in open environments tend to seek out essentially the same resources there as those they exploit when living in closed forest, it appears that some archaic ape lineages were prepared to be a little more flexible, and to explore the new opportunities the expanding mosaic of environments had to offer.

In the late Miocene some apes, most notably a handful of European forms living in deciduous forest and woodland environments, were already experimenting with new ways of moving around in the trees. One of them, the 45–65-pound *Danuvius*, an ape known from 11.6-myr-old fossils found in southern Germany, has been interpreted as an "extended-limb clamberer" that typically moved along the tops of larger tree branches on its hind limbs, while stabilizing its body by grasping smaller branches above. In contrast to this unusual form of arboreal locomotion, the dentition of *Danuvius* is pretty typical for an ape, with large upper canine teeth that honed against the front premolars below when the toothrows occluded. Something similar can be said for the slightly older Spanish *Pierolapithecus* which, in common with a small number of other European Miocene apes, also shows evidence of orthograde (erect) posture. One late Miocene European fossil that does have a short face and reduced canines more like those of humans is the 7–9-myr-old "swamp ape" *Oreopithecus* from Italy. But while *Oreopithecus* shows some anatomical indications of orthograde suspensory locomotion, and in addition had a hand reportedly capable of a humanlike "precision grip," its strange molar teeth are those of a specialized leaf-eater, and it remains in a category of its own.

The African fossil record has yet to produce any late Miocene fossil apes that document orthograde posture in the way the European forms do. But since the first bipedal hominins appeared in that continent, and remained confined there for several million years, there is little doubt that the pre-hominin ancestor lived in the forests of late Miocene Africa, and that when found it will bear at least some of the hallmarks of orthograde posture. That is because by now it is clear that erect posture and locomotion are the founding adaptations of the hominin subfamily, their indications being present in all plausible contenders for "earliest hominin."

Since we don't usually think of ourselves as peculiar, we take moving around on two legs for granted; but this is in fact a highly unusual way of getting about, basically shared only with birds and hopping mammals. But whereas birds actively recruited their forelimbs for flying, the arms and hands of ancestral humans became available for manipulating objects and other purposes simply as a by-product of walking around on two legs (and in the process, it's been suggested, inadvertently escaping from a "specialization trap" that seems to have ensnared other apes in a self-reinforcing feedback between diet, loco-motion, and cognition). So, why did an originally four-handed ape start habitually locomoting bipedally on the ground? Well, paleoanthropologists have come up with a lot of ingenious suggestions.

Charles Darwin started the ball rolling in his 1871 *Descent of Man*, in which he famously linked upright posture with the freeing of the hands from locomo-tion. Upright humans could not only make useful and aggressive tools, but they could hurl rocks at attackers, meaning that they no longer needed large canine teeth to defend themselves. Sophisticated cognition, larger brain sizes, and complex cultures then followed, in a self-amplifying cycle. This was a compelling story; but alas, as we now know, hominins had been upright for millions of years before they used their free hands to make stone tools. Not only that, but some modern apes use tools even though they are quadrupedal "knuckle walkers" who need to keep their long, slender hands folded into a fist while walking on the ground to protect their long, fragile fingers. Darwin was right about the canines, which are diminished along with the premolar honing mechanism in all putative early hominin bipeds. But it remains unclear what the exact relationship is between bipedality and the modified canine complex.

Well, if the key advantage of bipedality was not the freeing of the hands to make tools, what was it? Suggestions have been legion. One compelling notion was that the value of free hands lay not in making things, but in carrying them. Another was that by standing tall you could see predators from farther away, over the tops of tall grasses. But then, maybe physiology was more likely involved: Overheating is an ever-present problem in the tropics, and by standing up you present less of your body area to absorb the sun's rays, while also exposing yourself to cooling breezes. Or perhaps you expend less energy in the new terrestrial environment by moving around on two feet instead of four. Then again, if you are female with tiny offspring you can carry them around in your arms, even in the absence of the body hair that infants had previously clung to. Or, if male, you can indulge in more intimidating displays. Or in more effective bonding ones. And on and on.

But while some of these suggested key benefits to bipedality are inherently more plausible than others, all face the same objection: that to gain from any of them, you have to have stood upright in the first place. And once you have done that, of course, *all* of the advantages of bipedality – and also all of its *dis*advantages, including its excruciating slowness – are available to you. What is more, it is surely unrealistic to imagine that a quadruped would have come to the ground and then thought, "wouldn't it be nicer to stand up and see farther, or cool off better, or carry stuff?" That's because organisms simply do what comes naturally; and the only reason why a four-handed ape descending to the ground would have chosen bipedality, rather than ambling around on all fours – and fleeing rapidly should the occasion have demanded it – would have been that it simply felt most comfortable moving around on two feet. And that would only have been the case if it was already accustomed to holding its trunk upright in the trees – to an even greater extent than the suspensory living orangutan, which is a good facultative biped on the ground but nonetheless remains essentially a quadruped when there. And that brings us back to late Miocene forms such as *Danuvius*. The German fossil was almost certainly not a direct hominin ancestor; but as interpreted it nonetheless shows us what the ape radiation was capable of, and plausibly presents us with at least an approximate postcranial model for our own ancient African progenitor.

The Contenders for "Earliest Hominin"

Right up to the very end of the last century, the earliest putative hominin known was well under four million years old. Then, within the space of a decade, four new contenders appeared in the 4- to 7-myr time band. The most ancient of these is Chad's *Sahelanthropus tchadensis*, known thus far from a single crushed cranium (Figure 4.5, center), some partial mandibles, and maybe a partial femur. The associated fauna suggests that all these fossils are between 6 and 7 myr old, and they are placed at the older end of that range by cosmogenic nuclide dating (Chapter 2). *Sahelanthropus* initially appeared notable for a very small (350 ml) braincase and a flattish face; but a virtual reconstruction published in 2005 showed the face to have protruded quite strongly. The canine teeth were reduced, if pointy, and the squarish molar teeth were consistent with the cranium's hominin assignment. Most suggestive of bipedality was the presence underneath the braincase of a downwardly pointing foramen magnum. In contrast, a study in 2020 found the femoral fragment not to be that of a biped, casting doubt either on the association between the femur and the cranium (on which the authors insisted), or on the putative hominin's bipedality. The *Sahelanthropus* saga thus continues; but wherever in the family tree this form eventually turns out to belong, the fauna found with it suggests that it lived in a well-watered environment, with forest nearby.

Next in the timescale is *Orrorin tugenensis*, a medley of broken postcranial bones and bits of jaw and teeth from localities in the Tugen Hills of northern Kenya. They date from around 6 myr, and may or may not all belong to the same species. The molar teeth are squarish and thick-enameled, both hominin resemblances, and a canine tooth is pointed but small. The broken femora are consistent with bipedality. One could certainly wish for more, but this handful of fragments is strongly suggestive that a bipedal hominin was moving around on the open woodlands, interspersed with denser forest, that covered the northern Kenyan landscape around 6 myr ago.

Almost as old as *Orrorin* is *Ardipithecus kadabba*, an equally intriguing, fragmentary, and speculatively associated collection of fossils from sites in Ethiopia's Middle Awash region that date between 5.7 and 5.2 myr ago. Canines are smallish but distinctly pointed, and there appear to be lingering echoes of the canine–premolar honing mechanism. A toe bone from the younger end of the time range is said to show bipedal features.

Much better known is *Ardipithecus ramidus*, known from sites in the Middle Awash dating to around 4.4 myr ago. Fossils include a fairly complete though badly fragmented skeleton (Figure 5.1) that, after virtual reconstruction, has yielded a much more complete picture than we have for any other putative early hominin. A chimpanzee-sized cranial vault (300–350 ml) sat behind a sharply protruding but delicately built face that contained small and blunt canine teeth. These lay in front of squarish molars that, unlike those of later hominids, had a thinnish enamel coating. The vestigial honing mechanism seen in *A. kadabba* is gone. A short cranial base suggested a downwardly turned foramen magnum; and indeed, the describers specifically noted similarities to *Sahelanthropus* in this regard.

Below the neck, the *ramidus* team drew attention to features of the pelvis that might suggest bipedality; but surprisingly, although they found much to suggest that their subject had been a good climber, they did not find any specifically suspensory features. The approximately equal length of arms and legs suggested to them instead that the creature had adopted a very un-chimpanzee-like "palmigrade quadrupedalism" in the trees, while preferring an upright posture on the ground (Figure 5.1). But then there were the feet: long and lacking arches, and with a fully opposable great toe – the grasping feet of a climber. No other early hominin foot is like this. The habitats within which *A. ramidus* locomoted in its unusual way appear to have ranged from closed woodlands with denser forests nearby, to bushlands with some grasses.

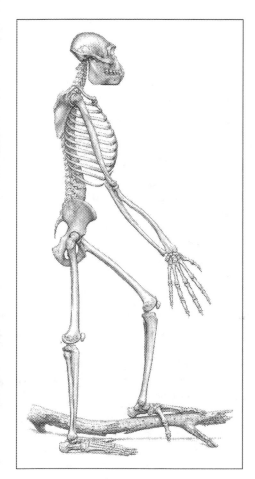

Figure 5.1 Reconstructed skeleton of *Ardipithecus ramidus* (NME ARA-VP 6/500), from Aramis, Ethiopia.

The final entrant in the "early biped" stakes, and the only one providing a reasonably direct connection to later hominins, is *Australopithecus anamensis*, described from northern Kenya in 2005 from 4.2- to 3.9-kyr-old specimens. These include upper and lower jaws that very broadly justify the *Australopithecus* appellation despite the long, parallel tooth rows; and a broken tibia (the large bone of the lower leg) had unquestionably belonged to a biped. Specifically, this bone showed signs of the telltale "carrying angle" that is formed when the femur slants inward from the hip to the knee. The tibia is consequently held vertically during locomotion, transmitting the body's weight directly down through the ankle joint, and allowing the lower leg to be swung forward in a straight line. Lacking this angle, a quadrupedal ape walking bipedally must inefficiently shift its center of mass from side to side as, with each step, it rotates its body around the supporting foot.

A damaged 3.8-myr-old cranium from Ethiopia's Woranso-Mille was described in 2019 as that of an *Australopithecus anamensis* (Figure 4.5, left). It had held a brain of a very modest 370 ml volume, and it had a heavily built face and a largish canine (for a hominin); but it seems reasonably attributed. It is, however, younger than the oldest known fragment of *A. afarensis*, the species into which *A. anamensis* was often said to have evolved. That means that the earlier species did not gradually evolve into the later one. Instead, the two coexisted for a significant stretch of time – although it is still believed that *A. afarensis* was ultimately derived from *A. anamensis*, via speciation. Various lines of evidence suggest that *A. anamensis* inhabited a complex mosaic of closed woodlands and more open bushlands with some grassland nearby; and a study in 2012 revealed that it had eaten an unexpectedly tough and very un-apelike diet that not only included the ancestral fruits and young leaves, but many of the resources only available in more open environments, such as tubers, seeds, grass rhizomes, sedges, and so forth.

So, what can we conclude about the origin of the hominin subfamily? We have several contenders for the title of "earliest hominin biped" in the 7 to 4-myr period, all laying claim in some way to canine reduction in addition to the novel upright form of locomotion. All were descended from more arboreal ancestors and probably foraged for resources outside closed forests and dense woodlands, although they presumably took refuge in the trees at night and when danger threatened, and opportunistically fed on the fruit they offered. They had ape-size brains and presumably broadly apelike cognitive styles, meaning that they were quite probably the smartest organisms of their time. As to the details of hominin emergence, analysis is complicated by the fact that nobody knows exactly what the stem hominin *ought* to have looked like (not surprising, because the closer a species is to the common ancestor of a group, the fewer derived features of that group it will show). None of the contenders prior to *Australopithecus anamensis* has a perfect claim to be hominin; and indeed, it is entirely possible that more than one lineage of orthograde arboreal hominoid may have responded to climatic and habitat stresses by descending at least part-time to the ground in search of sustenance, moving upright once there because of an ancestral orthograde proclivity. But one might equally adopt the perspective that incipiently bipedal descendants of the hominin ancestor were, from the very beginning, showing in their new environment the spirit of experimentation with the hominin potential that we see so vigorously expressed in later phases of human evolution.

The Australopiths

Numerous australopiths (*Australopithecus* and its close relatives) are by now known in the period between about 4 and 1.5 myr ago. They come from several different areas of the African continent: all the way from Chad in the west to the Afar Triangle in the east; from Ethiopia south along the Rift Valley through Kenya and Tanzania to Malawi; and of course from South Africa. From this diversity, wide distribution, abundance, and long duration alone, it is clear that the basic bipedal australopith body plan – involving smallish brains, reduced canines, large chewing teeth, short legs, and petite stature – was hugely successful; and it would be a big mistake to view it simply as a "transitional" stage between the apes and later humans. It clearly represented a durable and effective adaptive "response" to the new conditions that were spreading in Africa.

There is no space here to do proper justice to australopith variety, so let's select one well-known species as an exemplar. The obvious choice is the Ethiopian *Australopithecus afarensis*, because it is well documented, has been studied in some detail, and appears to be reasonably representative of its wider group. Following the discovery of the 3.2-myr-old Lucy and the 3.4-myr-old First Family fossils, it became quite common to refer to the australopiths as "bipedal apes"; but it is clear in retrospect that this epithet is a bit misleading. Like the other australopiths, *A. afarensis* was certainly a habitual biped when on the ground, but it nonetheless locomoted rather differently from later hominins. And while it had the large, jutting face of an ape, hafted in front of a small, ape-sized braincase, that face had housed a very different kind of dentition, and the base of the skull was radically modified for bipedality. This was neither an ape nor a human, but something distinctively different.

The Lucy skeleton is tiny; in life she had not stood much over three feet tall, though a 3.6-myr-old australopith from Woranso-Mille, attributed to the same species, was oddly long-legged and may have stood well over five feet. When Lucy was first discovered, attention naturally enough became focused on her clearly bipedal features. Her femur and knee joints clearly showed that carrying angle, for example, and her ankle had efficiently transmitted the body weight directly down to the foot. Lucy herself only preserved a couple of foot bones; but other fossils eventually showed that, although the *Australopithecus afarensis* foot had been relatively long and its digits slightly curved, it had possessed significant bipedal hallmarks. Bipedality was also clearly reflected in the Laetoli footprints, although the feet that made them had apparently been shorter and stouter than the still quite flexible foot reconstructed at Hadar. In 2018 researchers found that the foot of a 3.3-myr-old juvenile skeleton of *A. afarensis* discovered just across the Awash River at Dikika had a fairly mobile great toe, possibly due to its tender age. Still, all in all the foot of *A. afarensis* was that of a habitual biped, though indications are that its gait would have differed from our own. Something similar can be said for the *afarensis* pelvis which, in contrast to its long, narrow counterpart in the apes, is even broader and more flaring than its homologue in modern humans. At first this breadth was taken to indicate a kind of "super-bipedality," but it was later pointed out that it was a necessary compensation for the short legs, which would themselves have been an aid in climbing.

The upper body of *A. afarensis* emphasized the arboreal theme, although Lucy's arms were significantly shorter relative to her trunk than those of, say, a bonobo. Her rib cage tapered sharply upward, from a broad bipedal pelvis to the narrow shoulders of a climber whose shoulder joints faced somewhat up, rather than outward like ours. Hand bones found at Hadar indicate that *afarensis* hands were considerably shorter and broader than their longer and narrower equivalents in apes (providing greater manipulative potential); but the digits were slightly curved, and other features also suggest a powerful grasping capacity. Putting all these indications together, paleoanthropologists began to piece together a picture of *A. afarensis* as a hominin committed neither to the ancestral forests, nor to the open environments that lay in the future. Lucy and her kind probably foraged extensively on the ground, in habitats that ranged from closed forest through open woodlands to bushlands. But they still depended on the trees for sleeping and shelter (indeed, it's been suggested that Lucy herself died in a fall from a tree), and probably for a significant proportion of their diet as well. Microwear studies of *afarensis* teeth suggested a tough diet of items such as leaves and grasses (as opposed to the harder, more brittle diet of such things as nuts and seeds that was detected using similar techniques in the South African australopiths; the difference was almost certainly due environmental factors, emphasizing australopith versatility). Isotopic analysis of teeth more specifically suggested that *A. afarensis* preferred a diet of savanna-based foods such as sedges, grasses, and succulents – a preference that remained stable over time, albeit with wide individual variation. Once again, we are left with a picture of an adaptable opportunist that was equally at home on the ground and in the trees, and ready to take advantage of whatever its changing environment offered.

Australopith Behaviors

Just as we have a strong tendency to view our more recent ancestors as less-evolved versions of ourselves, we are often inclined to view the very early African hominins as evolved versions of today's African apes. And, as our closest extant relatives, the chimpanzees and bonobos might seem to be the obvious living models for our earliest precursors. However, these relatives not only differ behaviorally from each other but remain basically forest-bound creatures with long independent evolutionary histories since parting company with our mutual common ancestor at some point around 7 or 8 myr ago. My colleagues Donna Hart and Bob Sussman therefore proposed that the lives of slightly more remote extant primate relatives living in similarly open and dangerous environments, namely, the macaques and baboons, might give us more insight into how the early hominins organized themselves in their new and dangerous environments. And dangerous their habitats certainly were. In the deep forest, animals as large as apes would have had relatively few natural enemies. But out in the Plio-Pleistocene woodlands and bushlands, slow-moving and small-canined bipeds would have encountered a huge range of

Figure 5.2   Artist's impression of a leopard dragging a *Paranthropus* cadaver. Based on a cranial fragment from Swartkrans, South Africa, that bears twin holes almost certainly made by leopard canine teeth.

large-bodied predators against whom they were biologically defenseless. We are poignantly reminded of this by a piece of adolescent australopith skull from Swartkrans that has twin holes precisely matching the lower canine teeth of a leopard (Figure 5.2). Life was extremely hazardous away from the safety of the trees, in an environment patrolled by an alarming array of predators, including the fearsome sabertooth *Dinofelis*.

So, if the australopiths were actually prey species in their new environment, how would they have organized to minimize the risk to individuals? Hart and Sussman identified several strategies used by terrestrial monkeys today to cope with similar exigencies: live in very large groups, on the principle of safety in numbers; be as versatile as possible in your use of the environment (as we know the australopiths were); maintain a flexible social organization and be prepared to split up the larger group up as resources dictate; use males as sentinels, especially if they are significantly larger than females, as we know was the case with *Australopithecus afarensis* and the robusts; select your sleeping sites carefully on cliffs and in trees; stay during the day in the densest vegetation available, and if in the open maintain the largest subgroup size possible; and above all, be smart, especially about monitoring and reading the environment and communicating with each other. It is entirely reasonable to believe that the relatively large-brained australopiths would have unconsciously adhered to these principles as they moved into their new habitats – a far cry from the mighty hunters envisaged by Raymond Dart back in the 1950s, and from the pair-bonded social organization often envisaged by more recent paleoanthropologists.

Even though they had larger brains than the ancestral apes, this perspective makes the australopiths sound like fairly run-of-the-mill primates that were simply trying to accommodate to environments that were changing beyond their control. But at some point, they began to do something no primate had ever done before: They started producing stone cutting tools, presumably to make possible the butchery of animal carcasses. The first putative instance of such behaviors is provided by 3.4-myr-old cut-marked mammal bones from Dikika that were reported in 2010. The discovery of the first two examples at Dikika provoked a re-examination of the entire large collection of mammal fossils from the area, without producing any more. The second instance is those oddly large flakes reported in 2015 from the 3.3-myr-old Lomekwi 3 site in Kenya's West Turkana, still the only site from which such "Lomekwian" tools have been reported. At this point, both cases must be looked upon as outliers. But after the 2.6-myr point the story changes dramatically, as Mode 1 stone tools become a regular feature on the African landscape. There is no direct association between the very first stone tools and any particular hominin; but at Bouri in Ethiopia some cut-marked bones of 2.5 myr old were discovered close to the findspots of the fossils assigned to *Australopithecus garhi* (which some believe is a late *A. afarensis*). And in any event, at that point in time the only possible makers of stone tools were australopiths of one kind or another. This introduces a durable pattern in the archaeological record: namely, that the appearance of a new technology tends not to coincide with the appearance of a new kind of hominin. Which is entirely reasonable, of course, since any inventor of a new technology must belong to an existing species.

Making stone cutting tools placed the australopiths definitively beyond the documented cognitive range of apes. And it marks the beginning of the archaeological record, the material testament to past hominin behaviors. Prior to this, the only ancient behaviors we could know about were the few that could be inferred from anatomy; but now the spectrum broadened. We know, for example, that the early stone-tool makers had a capacity for forward planning that also lay outside the ape repertoire. Not all rock types are equally suitable for making tools, and since entire cobbles can be reconstructed from the flakes lying around at butchery sites, it is evident that the early lithics producers carried cobbles around with them in anticipation of needing them in places where good stone might not be found. The journey toward modern cognition had begun.

The early stone tools, and the carcasses they dismembered (as shown by cut-marks and bones smashed to extract marrow), provide the first evidence we have for regular hominin consumption of energy-rich animal fats and proteins. The highly opportunistic australopiths may, of course, have been doing this on a casual basis long before stone-tool making came along; after all, chimpanzees today often hunt smaller mammals – bushbabies in Senegal, mainly colobus monkeys in Tanzania – although they seem to share the carcasses for social purposes rather than for sustenance. But although the appearance of stone tools seems to signal the incorporation of animal products into the regular australopith diet, it is unknown whether and for how long carcasses were obtained by scavenging, rather than by active hunting. Still, because brain is an "expensive tissue" that requires a lot of energy to maintain, it is this qualitative enrichment of the hominin diet that seems to have set the stage for all the brain enlargement and cognitive developments that were to come.

Cognition

It is, of course, one thing to say that early hominins had moved beyond the ape level of cognition, and quite another to say exactly what that means. One possible starting point is with the sense of self and personal individuation. Modern humans can step back, as it were, and view themselves as distinct from the rest of nature. We consciously know what we know, and we understand that others, like us, have interior lives. The intellectual capacity that underwrites all this is our symbolic cognitive style. This term is shorthand for something we don't fully understand – and probably won't until we comprehend exactly how a mass of electrochemical discharges in the brain is transmuted into what we individually experience as our consciousness. But it does seem reasonably represented by the notion that we humans mentally deconstruct our interior and exterior worlds into a vocabulary of discrete abstract symbols. We can then rearrange those symbols, according to rules, to come up with new versions of those worlds – not only as they are, but as they *might* be. It is this that provides the basis for our imagination and creativity.

Apes – and all other organisms apart from us, as far as we know – lack this ability of ours to mentally recreate our surroundings and situations. They live in the world that Nature presents to them rather than in the world as reconstructed in the mind. Apes are cognitively sophisticated, of course; and they respond to stimuli in complex ways. They are, for example, apparently able like us to recognize that other individuals harbor beliefs, even false ones. But they apprehend such things at an *implicit*, intuitive, level, rather than at the *explicit* one that symbolic thought allows. And sadly, because like every other sentient species we *Homo sapiens* are prisoners of our own cognitive style, that is about as much as we can say at present. Whatever we might observe, we are unable to understand just what is going on in the mind of an ape. For the same reason, we have no way of accessing what it is subjectively like to *be* an ape – or for that matter an australopith, or any other fossil hominin. We can observe from the outside; but any picture we might come up with of how an ape sees the world – or, yet more dimly, of how fossil hominins saw theirs – will be so strongly filtered through our own symbolic way of understanding things that in the end it will be all about us, not about the ape or the fossil relative.

In many ways, the attempt to understand how an australopith manner of apprehending the world was eventually transformed into the symbolic cognition of modern humans is the subtext of the rest of this book. Meanwhile, what we *can* say is that later australopiths were capable of greater insights into the nature of the world around them than any creature before them. However inchoately, they recognized that the world could be manipulated, and not merely exploited for what it offered. What is more, the invention of stone tools was not only the foundational innovation of human technology, but proved to be the most consequential innovation ever, fundamentally changing the way in which hominins interacted with the world around them. It is currently impossible to know exactly how and when the biological underpinnings of the cognitive advance that lay behind all of this were acquired, still less what they were on the structural level. But by 2.6 myr ago the die was evidently cast, and hominins were off on a new and irreversible course.

6   The Muddle in the Middle

The Search for the "Earliest *Homo*"

Once Louis Leakey and his colleagues had described *Homo habilis* in 1964 the search for his Holy Grail of the "earliest *Homo*" was on, and the field was wide open for other entrants that had very little in common with *Homo sapiens*, the species by which our genus is defined. Genera are hopefully monophyletic collections of species descended from the same common ancestor; but there are no formal rules governing how inclusive they can be, so you could in theory create a monophyletic genus by including every primate on the planet. By unwritten convention, however, zoological genera are in effect the largest readily (I almost wrote "intuitively") recognizable unit, species being basically variations on the theme established by the genus. All species of the genus *Felis* are identifiably cats, and all *Rattus* are visibly rats. By this rule-of-thumb, as Bernard Wood and Mark Collard pointed out over two decades ago, the genus *Homo* should be confined to species that have significant resemblances to *Homo sapiens*. Just being related to the *Homo* clade, at some remove, is simply not enough. Such considerations are very important if you think that zoological classifications should somehow convey information about how the organisms in question are related.

But Leakey had opened the floodgates, and *Homo habilis* soon became the home for a motley assortment of fossils from various Rift Valley sites, in the 1.5–2.5-myr range, that their finders for one reason or another did not want to include in *Australopithecus*. Those who thought their discoveries distinct from *H. habilis*, but were too timid to name a new species, opted for the noncommittal *Homo* sp. The latest and most ancient entrant in this category is a mandible from Ledi-Geraru, just to the northeast of Ethiopia's Hadar. Dated to 2.8 myr ago, this specimen has an isotopic signature like earlier *Australopithecus* from the region, and it shows a suite of features in common with them as well as some claimed similarities to later *Homo*. The mandible certainly seems to provide evidence that there were at least two australopith lineages in the Awash Basin as the Pliocene was approaching its end; and it may even be the case that one of those lineages was related more closely than the other to the clade to which *Homo* belongs. But on its own terms the fossil hardly justifies being placed in our genus, and it provides a good example of how using a few more names would help clarify both the extent of taxic diversity and the actual geometry of events in human evolution.

Nobody doubts that the origin of the *Homo* clade is to be found somewhere within the prolific and very diverse australopith radiation. But where exactly is not clear: No known fossils fill the morphological bill for a transitional form. The late (2.0 myr) South African gracile australopith species *Australopithecus sediba* was recently touted as an intermediate, but it is in fact closely aligned with *A. africanus* and does not provide a substantial morphological link to the genus *Homo*. And indeed, if the origin of our distinctive genus is to be sought in a short-term event of genomic and developmental reorganization, rather than in a gradual transition, we may never find a form that does.

Maximum Muddle: "Early African *Homo erectus*"

I have borrowed the title of this chapter from the late great Glynn Isaac, who directed archaeological research in the Lake Turkana basin during the 1970s and early 1980s. By the "Muddle in the Middle" he was actually alluding to the emerging complexity of events during the middle Pleistocene throughout the Old World; but he might as well have been referencing the situation much closer to home. After the two largish-brained crania ER 3733 (Figure 4.2, lower left) and ER 3883 had been found at East Turkana in the middle 1970s, the moratorium on species names for *Homo* fossils found there was lifted. At 1.9 myr old (since adjusted to 1.6 myr), these two crania were the earliest known that comfortably fit the criteria for membership in *Homo* that Wood and Collard would promulgate a quarter-century later. And largely because of their comparable brain sizes (850 and 800 ml, vs. 900 ml), the Turkana team placed both specimens in Eugene Dubois's *Homo erectus* – despite their manifold differences in anatomical detail not only from each other, but even more from the million-year-younger Java skullcap that defines the Asian species. Regrettably, the resulting myth of "early African *Homo erectus*" still endures, although a growing number of paleoanthropologists prefers to call those forms *Homo ergaster*, using the name given to the 1.5-myr-old Ileret mandible by Colin Groves and Vratislav Mazak. That grouping is reasonable, at least on a provisional basis, and nobody has any problem with classifying those East Turkana fossils as early members of our genus *Homo*. In 1984, they were joined by the 1.6-myr-old "Nariokotome Boy" skeleton (Figure 6.1) from a site just across the lake.

Before we look at that astonishing West Turkana find in detail, it is worth noting that since the 1980s many more "early African *Homo erectus*" fossils have been discovered in eastern Africa. They include a smallish cranium from East Turkana's Ileret (1.55 myr; 691 ml), a 900-kyr frontal bone from a site in southern Kenya called Olorgesailie; a braincase from Daka in Ethiopia (~1.0 myr, 995 ml), and the cranium from Buia (also ~1.0 myr and 995 ml) in Eritrea. And then, of course, there is Louis Leakey's 1960 find of the Olduvai Hominid 9 calvaria (1.4 myr, 1,067 ml), plus a recently reported 2.0-myr-old partial juvenile braincase from South Africa's Drimolen site, best known for its *Paranthropus* fossils (there is a slightly younger contender for *Homo* status from Swartkrans, too). These specimens are very widely scattered across time and space, but what is even more remarkable about the group taken as a whole is its sheer morphological heterogeneity. Paleontologists in other subdisciplines would normally take such variety to indicate that early *Homo* was vigorously diversifying, spinning off new species as it explored the potential inherent in its new body form. But not paleoanthropologists; and it is a sign of the profession's terrifying insularity that, in ongoing obeisance to Ernst Mayr, so many of its practitioners still opt to brush all this disparateness under the shapeless rug of the ubiquitous and increasingly variable *Homo erectus*. Or, if you are heterodox enough, to cram it all into the single African species *Homo ergaster*.

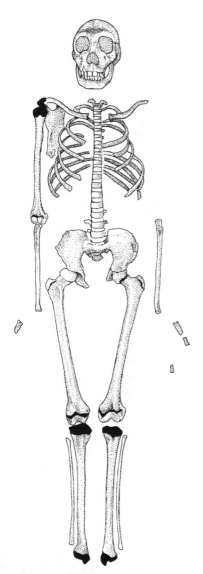

Figure 6.1   The KNM-WT 15000 skeleton of the "Nariokotome Boy" from West Turkana,

The Nariokotome Boy

The jewel of the Turkana Basin is undoubtedly the skeleton that is formally known as KNM-WT 15000, but more casually as the "Nariokotome Boy" (Figure 6.1) for his tender age and the site at which he was found. At the time, skeletons that came even close to the completeness of the Boy had been vanishingly rare in the pre-Neanderthal hominin record; but now at last it was possible to generate a reasonably complete picture of the earliest plausible *Homo* species (which, in the absence of an adequate systematic framework for early *Homo*, we'll call *Homo ergaster*). And it was a revelation! As described by the Leakey team, the Boy was remarkably modern, at least below the neck. The degree to which his teeth had erupted and his bones had fused, suggested that he had died at the developmental stage of a modern 11- or 12-year-old; and since he was already five feet three inches tall, the guess was that as an adult he would have topped six feet. Unlike the stocky, broad-in-the-beam australopiths, whose wide pelvises would have supported a large gut, he had been lean, with a narrow albeit still tapering thorax and a pelvis that was significantly restricted in width. What's more, compared to those of an australopith, his limbs, in particular the legs, were notably long and slender.

The Leakey team did note a few primitive features in the Boy. These included a constricted vertebral canal that suggested limited innervation of the chest area, and thus a lack of fine control of the airways and of sound production. The heads of his femora, the balls that fit into the hip sockets, were large, like ours, but they sat at the end of rather australopith-like long necks. Later studies have tended to emphasize the skeleton's archaic features. For instance, micro-imaging of his teeth suggested that the Boy had developed faster than a modern child does, and thus had died younger than first guessed, at a calendar age of maybe around eight years. One study suggested that he would have finished growing at the age of about twelve and a half, missing out on the modern adolescent growth spurt and adding only an inch or two of height. This is significant, because apes also develop much faster than humans do, limiting the period of social learning that is so critical for an animal that, as an adult, is so much what it has learned to be. For the record, australopiths seem to have developed on a fast schedule much more like that of apes than that of humans. Still, while the Boy's 880 ml brain would have expanded to only about 909 ml as an adult, that still places him ahead of the two approximately contemporaneous adult crania from the other side of Lake Turkana. His pelvic outlet was rather restricted, although this characteristic did not suggest that females of his species would have experienced obstetrical issues since newborn heads would not yet have been large enough to pose problems when passing through the birth canal. On the more modern side, a 2015 study concluded that the structure of the Boy's shoulder would have allowed him to hurl objects both accurately and far – something that apes, with their upwardly oriented shoulder joints, are not well equipped to do.

Even though he was nonmodern in some respects, then, the Nariokotome Boy gives us an image of a hominin radically different from that of the australopiths. We see above all a comparatively tall, striding biped, equipped for relatively effortless locomotion across the open savanna. So far, so good; but as we have seen, the savanna is a dangerous place. And in addition, far away from the shade of trees overheating would have been just as great a danger as any lion would have been. The brain, particularly, is exquisitely sensitive to heat overload; and in the absence of any specialized mechanisms for cooling it, a hominin's only option is to keep its entire body cool. A linear build like the Boy's would have helped in this by maximizing the heat-losing body surface area relative to its heat-generating interior. And his upright posture additionally minimized the area of his body directly exposed to absorbing the sun's rays, while maximizing the heat-radiating surfaces exposed to cooling breezes. But these things would not have been enough by themselves; and the "solution" arrived at by the hominins, most likely right at the origin of the genus *Homo*, depended on the power of evaporative cooling.

When it gets too hot human beings begin to sweat, exuding what is mainly water from the eccrine glands that are densely distributed over the body surface. As the sweat evaporates, it cools the skin as heat is used up in converting the tiny sweat beads into vapor. This is a very efficient way for hominins to lose unwanted heat, but it is impeded by a hairy coat such as our forest-living ancestors possessed: The sweat gets trapped in the hair and loses its evaporative power. It is therefore very likely that human ancestors lost their hairy covering (or, more properly, reduced it; we are still covered with microscopic hairs) at the point when they committed themselves to the open savanna and faced the problem of dealing full-time with the merciless tropical sun. But when you lose all that hair you expose your delicate skin to the sun's damaging ultraviolet rays, and some way of protecting it becomes necessary. The hominin "answer" is to load the skin's superficial layers with the dark, ultraviolet-blocking pigment known as melanin. And because all the factors just mentioned are functionally interlinked, it is a pretty good bet that the Nariokotome Boy himself had skin that was not only naked, but also darkly pigmented.

While the probably still quite hairy australopiths had been habitual bipeds on the ground, they retained a whole host of climbing adaptations. In stark contrast the Boy, doubtless descended not very long before from an australopith-like ancestor, was an obligate biped who had irrevocably left the forest canopy behind. This was an extraordinary shift, and exactly how that transformation was accomplished, or how long it took, are things that we cannot currently know. But it is very hard to imagine it as a slow, steady process that unfolded over the eons, as the savanna-dwelling proto-*Homo* became insensibly taller, longer-legged, darker, and less hairy; and indeed, that notion would seem to be contradicted by *Homo ergaster*'s abrupt appearance.

Life on the Savanna

Once *Homo ergaster* had committed itself to life out on the expanding and grass-dominated African savannas, it faced problems of survival very different to those that had confronted its woodland-living predecessors. From the material record, it is very hard to know exactly how these early *Homo* confronted those changes, because until about 1.6 myr ago (with a single outlier at 1.78 myr) the stone tools found mainly at butchery sites continued to be of the Mode 1 type that archaic hominins had already been using for a million years. Only at that point was a conceptually new type of stone tool introduced: the Mode 2 handaxe, a larger implement deliberately shaped on both sides to a predetermined (usually tear-drop) shape (Figure 6.2). Mode 1 toolmakers had simply been after a sharp cutting edge; it hadn't mattered to them what the flake looked like, so long as that edge was there. But Mode 2 tools were made to a template that clearly existed in the toolmaker's mind before knapping began, something that must reflect a cognitive advance of

Figure 6.2   A typical Acheulean handaxe. Scale is 1 cm.

some kind, even though it is hard to know how that advance would have been more generally expressed in *Homo ergaster*'s lifestyle. What's more, rather than being created when needed as Mode 1 tools were, handaxes were typically made in advance, sometimes in almost unimaginable quantities in what look like "workshops." And they were occasionally made in a playful or reverential spirit, too: at Isimila in Tanzania, for example, later hominins made huge but beautiful handaxes that were far too heavy to have been useful. But for a short while after *Homo ergaster* appeared the Mode 1 tool still reigned supreme, reinforcing the pattern established right at the start of the archaeological record: New tool types are not directly associated with new hominin species. Which meant, in this case, that the new body type had not depended on a new technology for its success, or even merely for its initial survival in the radically new environment to which its new physique had committed it from the very beginning.

Once adopted, the handaxe turned out to be an extraordinarily versatile tool that would continue to be made for well over a million years. Experimentation has shown that it is a very efficient implement for dismembering large carcasses, which brings us to the question of how much the new savanna lifestyle depended on hunting. The australopiths were almost certainly prey species, with lifestyles to match – even though, in their turn, they might occasionally have hunted small mammals while scavenging the carcasses of larger ones. And here is where questions of energy consumption enter the picture. Australopith brains had been, on average, perhaps one-quarter larger than those of apes of equivalent body size. But not until the genus *Homo* emerged did hominins start off on their notable trajectory of inexorable brain size increase. The Nariokotome Boy had a brain half as large again as that of an australopith, and by 1.5 million years later, hominin brains had doubled in size once more. Brains, as we have seen, are metabolically expensive to maintain; and larger brains, at any size level, could only be supported by improving the quality of the diet, most obviously by exploiting the animal fats and proteins that were the most rewarding resources the open savanna had to offer.

It is often imagined that before hunting had come scavenging, the exploitation of animals that had died of natural causes, or were killed by predators that had become satiated before completely consuming their prey. But there was stiff competition for nutrition of this kind from long-established scavengers, both aerial and terrestrial. And this is where those cutting flakes and handaxes may have come into play, allowing hominins to sneak in and rapidly detach parts of a carcass for consumption in some less dangerous spot. Alternatively, there was "power-scavenging," whereby hominins might have used their throwing prowess to hurl rocks and drive off competitors for carcasses. But whatever the exact strategy, scavenging would always have been a hazardous and problematic occupation. And since carcasses are found at unpredictable places on the landscape, scavenging would also have required the ability to locate them by observing indirect signs, such as vultures wheeling in the sky. All in all, once on the savanna there would have been a strong incentive to hunt one's own prey – even as one remained vulnerable to predation oneself. And although the hominins' lack of speed and slashing teeth made it impossible for them to compete with established predators and competitors on their own terms, their new body form offered them an entirely new style of hunting.

Human beings are slow, unable to outrun most mammals of any size over short distances. But what they do have in abundance is endurance. If they have enough water, members of *Homo* can walk or trot steadily all day long in the tropical heat. A colleague who worked at Hadar told me of his amazement when the local Afar tribesmen, hearing over the bush telegraph that the paleontologists had arrived, would walk 20 miles in the blazing heat to greet them, talk for half an hour, then get up and walk the 20 miles back, thinking nothing of it. Provided they had the ability to carry or access water, which is maybe not too much of a stretch to believe, this human ability to cover long distances, even in hot conditions, would have allowed hominins like the Nariokotome Boy to exploit a weakness in the physiology of the grazing mammals they saw all around them. Any one of those mammals could easily have outrun any hominins approaching them; but in the act it would have significantly heated up and would eventually have had to pause to pant away that heat, losing water as it did so. If the hominins doggedly followed their victim, the process would have repeated until, cheated of the opportunity to disperse its excess body heat, the overheated animal finally faced heatstroke and dehydration, and could no longer run away. At that point the hominins could simply have walked up and dispatched it; and, since it would have taken a while for scavengers to show up, they could have butchered it in peace. Louis Leakey is said to have tried this successfully, and it is an activity that would have required nothing beyond a rock for the final coup de grâce. Importantly, such hunting does not involve running fast, which is a dangerous thing for a biped to do on an uneven, unprepared surface: one twisted ankle or knee in an environment teeming with large predators might prove fatal.

Still, even if hominins did find their niche in endurance hunting, there is still the problem of how they digested the new diet. Compared to the australopiths, *Homo ergaster* showed significant reduction in the space available for its digestive tract. But it is vanishingly improbable that these hominins possessed any of the specializations for extracting nutrition shown by the short carnivore gut. This is significant, because while chimpanzees occasionally hunt and consume small mammals such as colobus monkeys, they seem not to gain much energy from this activity. Much of the flesh they eat is excreted undigested, even after a protracted passage through the intestinal tract. Almost certainly, hominins like the Nariokotome Boy would have faced a major problem in coaxing the energy required by their largish brains and very energetic lifestyles, even from a relatively rich diet that included animal products. One suggestion is that they increased the nutritive value of their foods by cooking them.

Cooking would have ameliorated the hominins' dietary problem in several ways. The primatologist Richard Wrangham has pointed out that cooking doesn't just make food taste better. It makes available otherwise indigestible nutrients, in both plant and animal foods. It softens those foods, making them easier to masticate even with significantly reduced chewing teeth and weaker jaws than those of the australopiths. And it also detoxifies them, which is a major consideration when you are eating carcasses that may have been rotting out in the sun for several days, or plant parts that might contain noxious defensive chemicals. Altogether, there is no doubt that cooking would have transformed unyielding and unappetizing resources into available and rewarding ones.

All of this is uncontestable, but where it runs into trouble is that cooking required fire. And there is precious little evidence to indicate that hominins had domesticated fire by two million years ago, or even by the time of the Nariokotome Boy, some 400 kyr later. There are a couple of indications that fires had burned at hominin sites dating from the 1.8- to 1.4-myr period, but these instances are very tenuous evidence for the controlled burning of cooking fires in hearths, which is first firmly documented at a South African site only about one million years old. And even then, we have to wait until well under 500 kyr ago before the intentional use of fire becomes anything like a regular feature at archaeological sites. Of course, fire use leaves a fairly fragile signal that might be expected to degrade with time; but if fire and cooking were key to the movement of hominins into the savannas, we might nonetheless reasonably hope for a better record of them. Still, the circumstantial case for early cooking is a strong one, and it is bolstered by the fact that fire would have been a potent protective weapon for open-country hominins threatened by predation. Not to mention that fire would have provided a focus for social attention and group cohesion, and might thus have provided a significant stimulus to the unusual prosociality of modern hominins. The jury has to stay out here, too.

Pending a better archaeological record for the first savanna-dwellers, we are largely in the realm of speculation about their lifeways. But it is hardly credible that the radical change of habitat did not somehow both reflect and precipitate a huge change in hominin life. A best guess views the australopiths as prey species that probably lived in high densities, and in large groups that lost many members to predation. In contrast, a similar guess sees *Homo ergaster* as apprentice hunters, secondary carnivores whose demographics rapidly came to resemble those of predators. Almost certainly, the mobile new high-endurance hominids lived in small groups that were thinly spread across the landscape and patrolled vast territories. Living as they did in an era of highly unstable environments during which local populations were regularly cut off from each other and subsequently recombined, they lived in a time that was ideal for the development of local variants. That in turn may explain the variety of morphologies currently included under the ecumenical rubric of *Homo ergaster*. It might also, conceivably, help explain the rapid increase in average brain size in the genus *Homo*, as the result of competition among species (yet to be acknowledged) in which an intuitive style of cognition evolved that scaled up in sophistication with increasing brain size. And it is a good bet that it helps account for the unusual prosociality of hominins, which is matched nowhere better than among those other social carnivores, dogs.

Leaving Africa

There are a few hints that hominins had left Africa and penetrated far-flung areas of both western and eastern Asia before about 2 myr ago. But the earliest well-documented hominin assemblage outside Africa comes from the 1.8-myr-old site of Dmanisi, in the Caucasus (Figure 4.6). In the conventional allocation of the Dmanisi hominins to what we might call the "*Homo erectus* group," we see at work a systematic mindset very similar to the one just described for the Turkana Basin and Africa in general. For a start, there is precious little justification for placing any of the small-brained Dmanisi hominins in the genus *Homo* (other than that they aren't *Australopithecus*). What's more, because they all come from the same site, the strong temptation has been to see all the Dmanisi hominins as members of the same species, whereas in fact they make up a very motley assemblage. Even if the first four Dmanisi skulls represent the same species, which some doubt, it is clearly stretching the bounds of credibility to force Skull 5 (Figure 4.6, left) into the same pigeonhole as the others, let alone into *Homo ergaster* (Figure 4.2, lower left). Had the fossils all been deposited in the sediments, like Hadar's First Family, in a single apparently instantaneous event, then one would have to strongly consider the possibility that all belonged to the same species. But that was not the case at Dmanisi, where the fauna accumulated over a long enough period – several centuries – for the site to have seen the passage of several different hominids exiting Africa via a well-defined Levantine land corridor. The makeup of the hominin assemblage from Dmanisi is thus as ripe for reappraisal as, back in Africa, the *Homo ergaster* wastebasket is.

Sadly, at historic rates of progress the current muddle will take several decades to sort out. So meanwhile, might it be more useful to ask just what it was that finally enabled hominins to exit Africa by about 1.8 myr ago, and in the process to penetrate significantly cooler and drier climes than they were used to? Unfortunately, answering that question in positive terms turns out to be harder than saying what the facilitating factor was not. It was not, for instance, the substantial increase in brain size we see in such individuals as KNM-ER 3733: Dmanisi brains were at the upper end of the very modest australopith volume range. It wasn't an improved technology, either: At Dmanisi the stone tools are all of Mode 1 type, basically indistinguishable from those that had already been made in Africa for half a million years. And neither was it self-evidently in greatly improved locomotion: The Dmanisi people had been short-statured, and reportedly had an archaic gait. So the jury must remain out on this key question, even as we grapple with such unknowables as the ancestry of the Flores hominin, which on morphological grounds might most plausibly have been derived from an even more archaic émigré from Africa.

Farther to the east, the earliest date for classic *Homo erectus* in Java has long been disputed. But new fission-track and uranium–lead dates, published in 2020, suggest that the Sangiran Dome area in which von Koenigswald worked, and from which the vast majority of Javan *Homo erectus* fossils have come, was first occupied by hominins only about 1.3 myr ago. The latest hominin-bearing deposits in the area are dated to about 0.7 myr, though fossils found elsewhere indicate that the mildly modifying *Homo erectus* lineage existed in Java until as recently as 117 to 108 kyr ago. As a result, unlike the Dmanisi hominins that are penecontemporaneous with the earliest *Homo ergaster*, it is possible to envisage that *Homo erectus* might ultimately have been descended from an early member of the *Homo ergaster* group, evolving its anatomical specializations once it had arrived in its southeast Asian redoubt. Fairly large numbers of flaked stone artifacts are known from Sangiran and elsewhere in Java, but they do not include the handaxes that were invented quite early in the tenure of the *Homo ergaster* group in Africa.

Putting all this together suggests that there were at least two migrations of hominins out of Africa in the period following about 2 myr ago; and maybe there was another even earlier, should it be established that the Flores hominin had acquired its anatomical peculiarities from a very archaically proportioned African antecedent. Most of the Java stone tools were found in secondary deposits, which means that we have no real "archaeological sites" for *Homo erectus* in the island, although indications are that this hominin lived in a humid and regularly inundated tree savanna environment very different from the desiccating African savannas that were roamed by *Homo ergaster*. This confirms that the fully bipedal *Homo erectus* was both rugged and adaptable; the Chinese representatives of the species that lived around Zhoukoudian some 770 kyr ago, for example, dwelt in a much more seasonal and temperate environment. The wide range of dates for Javan *Homo erectus* fossils provides us with the longest documented duration for a single hominin species, of almost 1.3 million years. There were some minor morphological differences among the samples of this species from different points in time, the most interesting intraspecies trend being in brain size, which increased from 813–1,059 ml in the earliest measurable specimens, to 1,090–1,251 ml in the latest ones. Extinction of this durable species, once widely spread in eastern Asia, probably came only after *Homo sapiens* had arrived in its homeland.

7 *Homo heidelbergensis* and the Neanderthals

Homo heidelbergensis

The morphological medley of hominin crania known in Africa following the one-million-year mark indicates that the subfamily's tendency to diversify continued unabated. It is frankly unclear exactly what was happening earlier in this period, but by about 600 kyr ago one hominin species had come to dominate the scene: *Homo heidelbergensis*. This was the world's first-documented cosmopolitan hominid, with representatives from France, Italy, and Greece (Figure 7.1, left) in Europe; from South Africa, Zambia (Figure 7.1, center), and Ethiopia in Africa; and from China in Asia (Figure 7.1, right), apparently including the recently ballyhooed "Dragon Man" cranium from Harbin that was dubbed *Homo longi*. Dating of many of the known specimens is poor, but plausible dates as early as 600 kyr have been claimed for *H. heidelbergensis* in both Europe and Africa; and, the Dragon Man (>146 kyr) excepted, no proposed date for the species is more recent than about 200 kyr. Most of the fossils that represent *H. heidelbergensis* are cranial, and present us with a picture of a heavy-boned form with a modestly sized dentition and a reasonably large brain of between about 1,166 and 1,325 ml. Its face is massive, surmounted by very high brow ridges that show a characteristic lateral "twist." Nothing like a complete skeleton of *H. heidelbergensis* is known, but the postcranial bones we do have are witness to a robust build, with a moderately wide pelvis and heavily built limbs of basically modern proportions. Allowing for flyaway hair and almost certainly some clothing in northern climes, on the landscape you would likely have had to approach to within a dozen yards of one of these hominids before clearly noticing that he or she looked rather different from you.

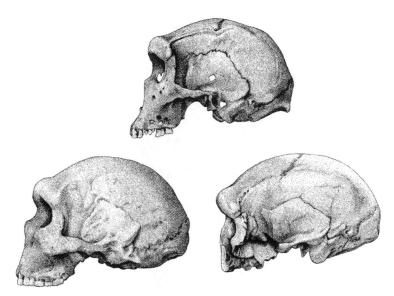

Figure 7.1   Three crania of *Homo heidelbergensis*, from Petralona, Greece (left), Kabwe, Zambia (center), and Dali, China (right). Not to exact scale.

You might also have noticed that they were brandishing some quite sophisticated implements, for during the tenure of *Homo heidelbergensis* several significant technological innovations were made. These included the first compound tools, with stone tips mounted into handles of softer materials. By making the tools easier to grip and providing greater leverage, such hafting vastly improved the efficiency with which the stone cutting and scraping components could be used. *Homo heidelbergensis* was also the putative maker of the first-documented artificial shelters, which include some quite large huts that were built on a beach in southern France some 380 kyr ago (Figure 7.2). Constructed by embedding slender saplings into the ground along the perimeter of a 10-meter-long oval, then presumably bringing them together in the structure's midline and covering them with hides, the largest of these huts shows a gap in the line of saplings that corresponded to the entrance. Just inside this gap, a fire with some charred bones had burned in

Figure 7.2 Artist's impression of the largest of the structures made some 380 kyr ago at Terra Amata, in southern France. Just inside the entrance, a fire had once burned in a scooped-out and cobble-lined hearth that contained burned mammal bones.

a shallow stone-lined hearth. As we saw, there is some spotty evidence for fire use earlier in the record, but it is really at this point that controlled fire begins to become a regular feature at camp sites.

Although those beach huts were probably not inhabited for long, they have huge resonances given how fundamental the notion of a "home" is for us today; and their invention surely has cognitive connotations. At the northern German site of Schoeningen, several carefully shaped wooden spears of comparable age were found that have all the essential characteristics of a modern javelin, with the center of balance toward the front. Given that wood rarely preserves, it is hard to know exactly when throwing spears were invented, and it's been noted that the wooden tips of the Schoeningen spears would have been of limited penetrating power; but the existence of these examples confirms that "death at a distance" was a reality by around 350 kyr ago, with everything that may imply for hominid intergroup (and maybe intragroup) relationships, as well for hunting prowess. That prowess was

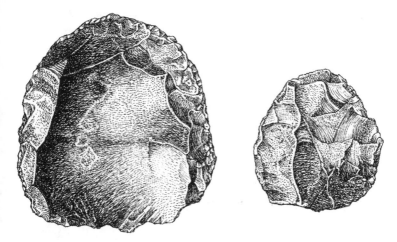

Figure 7.3   A Mode 3 core (left) and the flake removed from it, slightly modified by retouch.

evidently highly honed: in places, *Homo heidelbergensis* hunted some fearsomely large prey. It is also presumably significant that it was during the tenure of this species that the first conceptual revolution in stone working since the invention of the handaxe occurred. This was the introduction of the "prepared-core" (Mode 3) tool (Figure 7.3), in the manufacture of which a high-quality (predictably fracturing) stone core was shaped carefully on both sides until a single blow on a prepared platform would produce a semi-finished stone tool, or even a series of them with successive strikes. The double advantage here was that the flake had a continuous cutting edge all around its periphery, and that it could easily be transformed by further flaking, often using a "soft" hammer of bone or antler, into the exact form desired: an awl, or a scraper, or a knife.

All this makes clear that *Homo heidelbergensis* was a tough, resourceful, and clever hominin, with a significant cultural armamentarium and the ability to occupy and exploit a huge range of different environments. What its members do not seem to have possessed, is the symbolic capacity that so amply characterizes *H. sapiens*. This, it should be repeated, does not mean that they were not cognitively very complex. Many very sophisticated behaviors, including the production of some quite refined utensils, have almost certainly been mediated by elaborations of the ancestral intuitive hominin cognitive system, in which "intelligence," however defined, seems to have scaled directly with brain size. And that fact presumably accounts for the ultimate success of larger-brained species in the *Homo* clade. However, as the possessors of a symbolic cognitive system, we modern humans have difficulty imagining what it might be like to be extremely smart and capable, but not to be symbolic: not to live in the worlds we invent in our minds. And it is almost certainly into this category that *H. heidelbergensis* falls. Because, for all the remarkable things its members made and did, *H. heidelbergensis* only very arguably ever produced anything overtly symbolic; and it is only from explicitly symbolic items that we can reasonably infer symbolic mental processes.

The one putatively symbolic object known that might have been produced by *H. heidelbergensis* is a naturally shaped volcanic pebble that was found on the Golan Heights at a site dating to around 250 kyr. It is in the approximate form of a woman, and it may (or may not) have been slightly altered to improve that resemblance. But one swallow doesn't make a summer; and the probability is that any creature that reasoned symbolically would have left much more substantial evidence of that proclivity. To provide perspective, the only possibly symbolic manifestation older than this one is a single mollusk shell, some 500 kyr old, that was found at Trinil in Java, and is putatively associated with *Homo erectus*. It bears some zig-zag markings that seem to have been deliberately made; but a similar caveat applies in this case as well. Both *H. erectus* and *H. heidelbergensis* were very smart creatures for their time, and it might even be surprising if an individual belonging to one of the two species had not occasionally done something that anticipated later developments. There is, however, a significant difference between occasional and unusual behaviors, and those that are the embedded properties of a society.

Who Were the Neanderthals?

Homo neanderthalensis is the best documented of all extinct hominin species. It was the fruit of a long-established European hominin lineage that may have gone all the way back to *Homo antecessor* at 780 kyr, and that is definitely

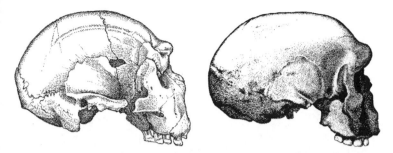

Figure 7.4 Left: the most complete of the crania (Sima 5) from the Atapuerca Sima de los Huesos site. A precursor of the Neanderthals, it has been suggested to belong to the same species as the cranium from Steinheim an der Murr, Germany (right), for which the name *Homo steinheimensis* is available. Not to exact scale.

represented some 430 kyr ago in the Sima de los Huesos site at Spain's Atapuerca. The Sima is where those 28 fragmented individuals were found at the bottom of a vertical shaft inside a cave, bereft of any archaeological context save one singularly beautiful handaxe. The Sima people share many features of the face (Figure 7.4) that align them with the Neanderthals, although the rear of their skull was less specialized. They had smaller brains, with a mean volume of 1,241 ml. Their postcranial structure was also more or less what you might expect for a Neanderthal precursor, showing robust skeletal build, broad pelvic flare, and a mean stature of 5 feet 6 inches that was slightly above the Neanderthal mean of around five feet four inches. A partial mitochondrial genome derived from a single Sima femur yielded a surprise in 2013, showing closer relationship with Denisovans than with Neanderthals; but two nuclear genomes reported in 2016 both revealed in contrast that "the Sima de los Huesos hominins were related to Neanderthals rather than to Denisovans." However, a mitochondrial genome from one of the specimens "share[d] the previously described relationship to Denisovan mitochondrial DNAs, suggesting ... that the mitochondrial DNA pool of Neanderthals turned over later in their history." The Neanderthal/Denisovan plot thus continues to thicken.

However the genomic story may eventually play out, there is ample morphological justification for placing the Sima fossils in their own species as a "sister" to the Neanderthals, or possibly even as a direct antecedent. What should that species be called? The Sima researchers first classified their fossils as *Homo heidelbergensis*, which was clearly incorrect and proved to be a huge stumbling-block to understanding exactly what was going on among the hominins of Middle Pleistocene Europe. The team has since recanted, but without saying what their fossils should be called. They are apparently reluctant to give the Sima people a new name because they consider it possible they belong to *Homo steinheimensis*, a species created in the 1930s to contain a distorted skull discovered in a gravel pit at Steinheim an der Murr in southern Germany (Figure 7.4). So, although the date of the Steinheim fossil is very broadly estimated at between 350 and 250 kyr ago, it is convenient to use this designation for the Sima material pending proper morphological analysis.

The distinctive species *Homo neanderthalensis* made its appearance at about 200 kyr ago, initially in Germany and soon thereafter in France; and by now Neanderthal fossils are known at localities stretching west–east all the way from the UK to southern Siberia's Denisova Cave, and from Wales and Denisova in the north to Spain's Andalucía in the south. The Neanderthals' characteristic Mode 3 Mousterian stone tool kit is found more widely yet; and this vast distribution is by itself testament to the Neanderthals' flexibility and adaptability in climatically unsteady times, although they apparently avoided the most extreme environments.

Below the neck the Neanderthals were fairly standard-issue Middle Pleistocene hominids, with strongly built skeletons that included thick-walled long bones and wide pelvises below rib cages that tapered notably upwards, although the shoulders were quite broad (see Figure 8.2, left). Neanderthal skulls, on the other hand, were highly diagnostic (Figure 7.5). Large cranial vaults enclosed brains averaging 1,497 ml in volume, but were wide and low with a characteristic rounded protrusion ("bun") at the back. The ample face, hafted in front of the braincase, had a large nasal region and sharply retreating cheekbones below orbits that were surmounted by rounded brow ridges that arced independently above each eye. Neanderthals also lacked the distinctive chin of modern humans, which is not simply a bump where the two sides of the lower jaw come together, but a complex reinforcing structure with several components that buttress the point of fusion. Because

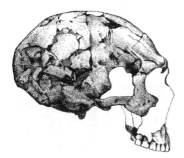 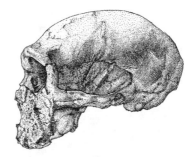

Figure 7.5 Two Neanderthal crania, from Amud in Israel (left), and Monte Circeo in Italy (right). Not to exact scale.

the Neanderthal face protruded a lot more than ours, that fusion point is reinforced in them on the inside of the mandible, rather than at its front. Unsurprisingly for such a well-known species, there is a lot of variation in skull morphology among known Neanderthals both in time and in space (the late northwestern European "classic" Neanderthals showed the characteristics of the species in a more exaggerated form). Nonetheless, wherever they come from, Neanderthals are all readily recognizable as members of the same group (Figure 7.5).

Recent work has also shown that the Neanderthals did not develop exactly as modern people do. They did not grow up as quickly as the Nariokotome Boy did, but they were on a faster schedule than we are. The upper third molars of Neanderthals, for instance, began to develop at a chronological age of under six years, three years earlier than they do in us. This and other indicators suggest that Neanderthals might have had a shorter period of infant dependence than we do, and that they may have acquired sexual maturity earlier, giving them a relatively abbreviated period in which to learn the complexities of social and economic existence. Recent studies have also shown that the features of the Neanderthal face followed very different growth trajectories from ours, and that those trajectories were already established at birth. Biologically, then, the differences between *Homo sapiens* and *H. neanderthalensis* were considerable, even if they were insufficient to impede the production of offspring.

As we saw in Chapter 4, despite those pronounced differences the genomic evidence now suggests that interbreeding between Neanderthals, Denisovans, and the incoming *Homo sapiens* happened quite frequently in Europe. A 2021 analysis of very early European *H. sapiens* crania from Bacho Kiro in Bulgaria (~44 kyr) showed some 3.4–3.8 percent Neanderthal ancestry, about twice as high as in Europeans today, while an individual from Zlaty Kun in the Czech Republic (probably over 45 kyr) was around 70 generations, or not more than 3,000 years, away from a Neanderthal ancestor. Interestingly, none of these individuals showed any special relationship to later Europeans, suggesting that the very early European *Homo sapiens* were pretty comprehensively replaced at some later point. For want of evidence, just what the broader social relationship between the Neanderthals and the incoming modern humans might typically have been remains entirely a matter for speculation. Given that the African *H. sapiens* and the Eurasian Neanderthals shared what by evolutionary standards was a pretty recent common ancestry, we should not be surprised by the finding of gene interchange between the two. But that compatibility would almost certainly not have greatly affected the grim reality that the newcomers and the Neanderthals would have been in competition for the resources available on a landscape that the moderns clearly exploited significantly more intensively than the Neanderthals ever had.

This latter reality is clearly expressed in the fact that, once modern humans had begun to flood into Europe at some time around 45 kyr ago, the always more sparsely distributed Neanderthals rapidly vanished. And they went extinct recognizably as themselves, while *Homo sapiens*, its physical peculiarities also intact, went on to take over the world. The latest date for Neanderthal survival is still debated. Iberia was once thought to be the last Neanderthal refuge; but with some key southern Spanish Neanderthal sites having now been shown to be older than believed, and a remarkably early 43 kyr date for early moderns at the Bajondillo cave in Andalucía, this is looking less likely. One current front-runner for the Neanderthals' last redoubt is a remote Siberian locality called Byzovaya, in the Ural Mountains a mere 100 miles south of the Arctic Circle. A stone tool assemblage some 31 kyr old at this site is said to be the handiwork of Neanderthals, though some prefer to withhold judgment on that attribution pending confirmation through DNA or fossil morphologies. What is uncontestable, though, is that as dating becomes more precise, the number of Neanderthal sites clearly dated to under 40 kyr ago is significantly shrinking.

The exact reasons for the rapid disappearance of the Neanderthals make for uncomfortable contemplation, for although we have virtually no evidence that bears directly on the nature of the interaction between the Neanderthals and moderns, it is extremely difficult to entirely exculpate *H. sapiens* in this matter. The Neanderthals may already have been thin on the ground when *H. sapiens* arrived in their territory; but they had successfully navigated numerous climatic and environmental vicissitudes for many tens of thousands of years, and those incoming modern humans were the only truly new element in the equation.

Neanderthal Lifeways

We surmise that Neanderthals lived at low densities, and in relatively small groups, because the occupation sites they left behind are not only usually smaller than those left on the same landscapes by later *Homo sapiens*, but also much less abundant. Guesses as to the average size of a Neanderthal social group have typically been of around a dozen individuals, which was about the size of a party, consisting mainly of adolescents and children, that left its (broad) footprints on a beach in Normandy some 80 kyr ago. However, in 2020 a set of Neanderthal trackways made around 100 kyr ago on a paleo-beach in southern Spain yielded a much larger minimum count of 31 individuals; 7 of them were children, 15 were adolescents, and 9 were adults. Some of the juveniles had been jumping around, evidently playing in the sand. This high count is still an outlier, however, especially in view of the one Neanderthal fossil assemblage that has been interpreted as representing an entire social group. This is the extraordinary finding at the northern Spanish cave of El Sidrón.

At El Sidrón, which dates to about 49 kyr ago, a collection of Neanderthal fossils was discovered that appears to have been deposited in the cave in a single event that likely involved the collapse of the ground surface or higher cave floor above. Numerous stone flakes were also found mixed in with the debris from the fall, and some of them could be remounted back into complete cobbles, indicating the tools had been made on the spot. The broken-up Neanderthal remains represented six adults, three adolescents, two juveniles, and an infant. All were apparently dead before the collapse occurred. After rejecting all other possibilities, the researchers concluded that the Neanderthals had been the victims of a massacre, since many of the bones showed signs of cutting and smashing consistent with intentional defleshing – and most likely with cannibalism. This behavior was probably not unusual among Neanderthals (and historically it has been less rare among modern humans than most of us would like to think), although the El Sidrón researchers noted that, unlike the "gastronomic cannibalism" seen at such sites as Atapuerca's Gran Dolina, in which habit rather than necessity was probably involved (because the overall population seemed well fed), here they were looking at the victims of "survival cannibalism" that was done out of necessity (because the population showed anatomical signs of dietary stress). The El Sidrón Neanderthals, the researchers decided, had lived in tough times during which one Neanderthal group had been ambushed, murdered, and eaten by another.

The idea that a single social unit was represented at El Sidrón is supported by genomic analyses which showed that all three males had belonged to the same mtDNA lineage, while each of the females had belonged to a different one. This suggests that the males formed the core of the group while females married out, leaving their natal group for another once they had reached puberty. When this information was first published, one colleague commented to the press: "I cannot help but suppose that Neanderthal girls wept as bitterly as modern girls faced by the prospect of leaving close family on their 'wedding' day." And she might well have been right. The idea of female exogamy was, by the way, supported by recent nuclear DNA results from the Denisova cave. The El Sidrón mtDNA study also showed that one 5–6-year-old and one 3–4-year-old were offspring of the same mother, suggesting a birth interval of about 2–3 years, comparable to what was historically seen among modern hunter-gatherers, and possibly implying extended birth spacing through late weaning. There are also clear suggestions that, however tendentious intergroup relationships may have on occasion become, there was substantial caring within Neanderthal groups. The most famous evidence for this comes from Shanidar Cave in Kurdish northern Iraq, where the skeleton of an aged (for a Neanderthal: 40-plus years) male shows that its owner had lived a long time with an amazing array of handicaps: one arm was withered or had been amputated, he had a deformed shoulder, and showed evidence of head wounds sustained over a long period. One of those wounds would have rendered him at least partially blind, and bony growths in his ear canals presaged deafness. Without the constant support of his group he could never have survived to be killed by a rockfall in his old age.

The Neanderthals also practiced less-alarming forms of corpse disposal than the one we see at El Sidrón. Indeed, one major reason why we have such a good fossil record of Neanderthals is that they at least occasionally buried their dead, perhaps the first hominins ever to do so. Their motives for this are impossible to know, although it is fair to point out that there are more practical reasons for burial (discouraging scavengers at living sites, for example) than the rather abstract ones that impel modern humans to a huge variety of funerary practices that only have in common a ritual context and, usually, belief in an afterlife. And there is very little apart from the act of burial itself to indicate that Neanderthal interments reflected the myriad motives that our symbolic capacities make possible: artifacts, for example, are at best rare in Neanderthal graves, and if present they are usually the kind of thing that might anyway have been lying around on the cave floor, to be accidentally shoveled in. It is also important to note that bodies were often not buried intact. Many Neanderthal bones show evidence of cadaver processing that included defleshing and the removal of body parts. An entire litany of Neanderthal mortuary practices of this kind has been described, and the fact that they were so often repeated suggests established practice, if not ritual. But those who carried them out evidently did not process information and feelings in exactly the same way that we do – recall that relative deficiency in genes for self-control and self-awareness we mentioned in Chapter 3 – so that what exactly those activities meant to those who performed them is impossible for us to imagine.

A complex motive for the El Sidrón massacre, rather than a purely dietary one, may be suggested by the stone from which the tools found at the site were made. This material was not available locally, and its nearest source was several miles away. The El Sidrón researchers suggested that obtaining it might have involved penetrating the territory of another group, whose consequent lust for retribution might have led to the carnage at the cave. That remains speculation; but it was certainly the case that good stone-working materials were hugely valued by the Neanderthals. That's because their Mousterian lithic tradition, a Mode 3 technology, depended on the availability of stone that fractured very predictably. Nondescript tools could be made from almost any stone, but any self-respecting Neanderthal toolmaker vastly preferred to use the right raw materials, which often had to be brought in from far afield and might even have been trade items. A tool made from a kind of stone that would both yield and hold a sharp edge was highly prized; and such implements were often resharpened again and again, until they were too small to grip any longer. And even then, they could be hafted into spear tips (apparently more often thrusting spears than throwing ones), using a pine or birch resin. The Neanderthals were, then, very skilled craftsmen in stone, perhaps making it surprising that they relatively sparingly used other materials such as the bone and antler that the Upper Paleolithic modern humans who replaced them liberally employed. But then again, while the Neanderthals made their tools with great skill, they didn't make them with the spark of creativity that so clearly characterized the work of the Upper Paleolithic folk. Several different traditions have been identified within the Mousterian – which was, after all, produced over a vast span of time and space, and certainly showed responses to changing conditions – but they were mostly variations on the same theme, whereas the Upper Paleolithic was above all about innovation.

Ironically for a group of Neanderthals whose bodies evidently furnished some conspecifics with a hearty meal, it turns out that the El Sidrón hominins had been vegetarians. A 2017 study of genetic material preserved in the calculus deposits on their teeth suggests that they subsisted on a diet of wild mushrooms, pine nuts, and moss, with no signs of any meat. If the same could be said for their attackers, that might explain a lot. One of the El Sidrón males had been afflicted with a painful dental abscess and a gastric bug, and he seems to have medicated himself not only with the penicillium fungus, but with poplar bark that contains the active ingredient of aspirin. The meatless diet was altogether unanticipated for Neanderthals, who were already documented by other means to have been formidable hunters of large mammals. It was thus perhaps comforting, then, that the DNA results reported at the same time for dental calculus on Neanderthal teeth from the Belgian Cave of Spy

(~40 kyr) were much more in line with expectation. The Spy Neanderthals had eaten not only the meat of mountain sheep and some large-bodied grazers, but also of wooly rhinoceros, with only a small side of mushrooms. Other studies make it clear that the Neanderthals typically not only hunted the full size-range of mammals available to them wherever they were (including occasionally big carnivores), but also butchered them systematically and with great skill.

Still, the contrast between the El Sidrón and Spy Neanderthal diets confirms just how flexible and opportunistic Neanderthal dietary strategies were. The Neanderthals lived in a lot of different places, and they ate whatever was available. One study in western Italy, for example, found that at around 120 kyr ago, during a warm phase, the Neanderthal occupants of a local cave had brought in the scavenged heads of older individuals that had probably died from natural causes. During colder times, some 50 kyr ago, the animal remains left by Neanderthals in a neighboring cave were entirely different: a miscellany of body parts, from animals in the prime of life that had probably been hunted. The latter diet was probably the one preferred, since we can infer a meat-heavy diet from the bone assemblages we typically encounter at Neanderthal living sites (though we shouldn't forget that plant materials rot quickly, biasing our perceptions); and now we can infer something similar from stable isotopes as well. Recall that the ratio between the two nitrogen isotopes ^{15}N and ^{14}N increases slightly in animal tissues the higher up the food chain you go; and nitrogen isotope studies in the 1990s showed that the bones of Neanderthals always had higher ^{15}N /^{14}N ratios than herbivores from the same place. Indeed, they were typically right up there with hyenas, lions, and wolves. In 2005, French researchers discovered an extraordinarily high ^{15}N /^{14}N ratio in a very late Neanderthal from a site in western France. So high, indeed, that it could only have been achieved by eating animals that were themselves enriched in ^{15}N; and those happened to be the most intimidating animals of all: wooly mammoths and wooly rhinoceroses. What is more, the researchers reckoned that a diet of this kind could only have been achieved by actively hunting those formidable prey species, because scavenging just would not have done the trick for a hominid with such an energy-intensive lifeway. More recently, it has transpired that Neanderthals living near the shore in Italy and southern Spain also collected live clams, in circumstances that possibly involved diving for them. They would certainly have consumed the clams before using their shells as scraping tools. Once more, the signal is of impressive versatility.

The Neanderthals occupied a vast range of territories and climatic conditions, many of them notably chilly. They were relatively stockily built, but these body proportions would not by themselves have protected them against extremes of cold. It was once calculated that Neanderthals would have required a layer of subcutaneous body fat almost equivalent in weight to the rest of their bodies to survive the worst periods of cold without clothing – and massive surplus body weight would, of course, have spelled doom for creatures with so highly energetic a lifestyle (it's been estimated that under the most extreme conditions a Neanderthal would have expended more than twice as many calories daily as an average modern person). That Neanderthals did wear clothing is supported by a curious form of wear on their front teeth that almost certainly resulted from using them to hold animal hides while scraping them. One of the uses of those hides would certainly have been in making some form of apparel, presumably held together by animal sinews that were passed through holes pierced with pointed stone flakes. Another way of keeping the cold at bay, as well as of cooking foods to make nutrients maximally available, was the control of fire in hearths. Such fires were routine features of Neanderthal occupation sites, which may well have been enclosed by hides for insulation. In some cases, structures may have been yet more complex: In one famous instance a circular enclosure was made by early Neanderthals deep within a cave in southwestern France, using broken stalactites and stalagmites. Light would have been required for this purpose, and there are also traces of burning that hint at something that went beyond simple illumination. Neanderthal structures inside caves may actually be a more common phenomenon than was thought (when it is really cold outside, deep caves, though dark, are relatively warm), and organic-rich layers in caves that hosted Neanderthals may represent the remains of ancient bedding – something that is documented in Africa back to 227 kyr ago.

All of this leaves the inescapable impression that the Neanderthals were highly capable and generalist hunters and gatherers who knew their environments intimately, and who were readily able to adjust their subsistence and domestic strategies according to the demands of both geography and climate.

Their material culture helped them to deal with climatic extremes, as well as providing sophisticated hunting equipment that was doubtless used in concert with clever hunting techniques. Some believe that, by the time *Homo sapiens* showed up in their territory, the Neanderthals were already dwindling and on the path to extinction. But the Neanderthals' flexible strategies had served them well in the past, and it is hard to believe that over much of their vast range they would not have found adequate ways of dealing with any climatic vicissitudes. The problem almost certainly lay elsewhere, with a new and qualitatively different competitor.

Neanderthal Cognition

So, what kind of creature was *Homo neanderthalensis*? What would it have been like to meet one? Despite the efforts of the novelists who are best placed to speculate about this, we really have no idea how the Neanderthals perceived the world or how they interacted with each other (or with us, when *Homo sapiens* finally showed up – what a moment to be a fly on the wall!). This is our fault, not theirs; as already noted, we are captive to our own cognitive style, and anything we might conclude about the Neanderthals will inevitably have been filtered through our own symbolic way of seeing things, which is a huge impediment to imagining what it was subjectively like to be a Neanderthal. What we can safely say, though, is that Neanderthals were not just an alternative version of ourselves. Instead, they seem to have embodied the most sophisticated expression on record of the ancestral, intuitive, style of hominin cognition, in which "intelligence," however one might wish to define it, probably scaled up more or less directly with raw brain mass. The behavioral benefits conferred by such intuitive, nondeclarative, intelligence had very plausibly underwritten the metabolically expensive long-term parallel trends toward expanding brain size in the genus *Homo*: trends that we see happening independently in three separate lineages within our genus, in Africa, in Europe, and in eastern Asia. But while in one African branch of our genus the symbolic reasoning of *Homo sapiens* eventually emerged from the local version of this larger tendency, it clearly did not do so as a simple extension of it. Symbolic reasoning is qualitatively different from the ancestral cognitive style, and its evolution was clearly not driven in the same way.

We can't say much from the external form of the large Neanderthal brain about what was going on inside it. As even a glance at the difference between the tall, globular braincases of modern humans, and the long, low ones of Neanderthals will tell you, there were some striking differences in overall brain shape. These were mainly due to a relative elongation of the Neanderthal brain, to the large visual areas at its rear (Neanderthal orbits were relatively large, too), and to a flattening which limited the volume of the prefrontal regions that are implicated in planning and other complex cognitive functions. The Neanderthal cerebellum was also smaller than its counterpart in *Homo sapiens*, suggesting possible differences in coordination and attention. But such disparities are hard to interpret in the context of overall brain function, as also are some indications of differences in brain development. As a result, our main source of information on Neanderthal cognition will continue to be the archaeological record – which is witness to considerable behavioral complexity. We have already seen how archaeological evidence suggests a high level of flexibility in Neanderthal subsistence strategies, along with great skill in certain activities demanding precise hand–eye–brain coordination and insight into the material properties of stone. And there are some intriguing issues of detail as well.

Principal among these are various putative indications that Neanderthals used symbolic information processing. This is a tough issue, not least because scientists vary in the kinds of manifestation they will accept as reflections of symbolic mental processes. Some, for example, might take the presence of ground ochre (a reddish pigment derived from common iron oxides) at an archaeological site as such an indicator; and ochre has been reported from numerous Neanderthal sites in Europe. Among modern hunting and gathering peoples, ochre has been employed as a food preservative, to repel insects, for bodily decoration, and in treating animal hides; and its most famous use, of course, was as a major pigment in the astonishing cave art of the Upper Paleolithic. Its occurrence at an Ice Age site might thus have been in any of these contexts, most of which are purely functional and thus do not give us prima facie evidence of symbolic intent (though cave art clearly would). Accordingly, it is dubious that ground ochre is by itself a bellwether for symbolic behavior; and indeed, in Africa ochre use pretty clearly began in nonsymbolic contexts, to be co-opted only later in symbolic ones. Much the same thing can be said, by the way, for the manufacture of stone tools, even complex ones. Since the making of any stone tool is far from easy, many observers have been tempted to see in the mastery of such technologies at least an incipient expression of the modern human style of intelligence; and it's even been argued that language would have been necessary for teaching stone working. But the reality is that "smart" and "symbolic" are far from synonyms, just as the difference between intuitive and symbolic intelligence is not just one of degree. An informal experiment in Japan showed that students learned how to make Mousterian points at similar rates, regardless of whether or not visual demonstration of technique was accompanied by verbal explanation.

Bodily decoration poses a difficult issue in this context, especially since among modern humans it is almost invariably bound up in symbolic overtones of group or class membership, or simply of taste. Wear jewelry as a member of our species, and you are making a statement about yourself, like it or not. And irrespective of whether Neanderthals ever used ochre to paint their bodies, it seems to be quite well established that, once in a long while, they did make decorative items. One example of this comes from the 130-kyr-old Neanderthal site of Krapina in Croatia, where several white-tailed eagle talons seem to have been nicked for stringing, presumably in a necklace or something similar. Some collagen fiber found in one of the nicks was probably a remnant of the binding; and although there is no record that the talons were associated with each other (the site was excavated at the turn of the twentieth century), the proposed decorative intent does seem plausible. Its probability is enhanced, moreover, by the aesthetic sense that Neanderthals seem to have possessed: they collected such items as seashells, fossils, and eye-catching minerals, sometimes carrying them considerable distances across the landscape. But does aesthetic appreciation equate to symbolic thought? Probably not. True, the quality of our own aesthetic experience today is hugely affected by the symbolic way in which we process our sensory inputs; but even in the absence of this special mode of dealing with information, the basic appreciation of symmetry and beauty would almost certainly have been there in some form. Indeed, it might have been no less powerful for being intuitive, with fewer layers of processing in between the observer and his or her emotional response.

There are plenty of other hints of inchoate complexities in Neanderthal life. These include inscrutable markings made on pieces of bone and stone, including the chevron pattern incised on a deer bone from the German Einhornhöhle cave that was announced with much fanfare in 2021. And they may even embrace ochre pigment daubings on cave walls. In 2018 scientists dated some markings on deep cave walls in Spain – none of them qualifying as representative art – to as much as 65 kyr ago: a time when only Neanderthals are known to have been in the region, and over 20 kyr earlier than any other dated cave-wall painting. The dating method – thorium–uranium on the thin calcite covering that has accumulated on top of the markings since they were made – is very recently developed, and in the eyes of some it is still experimental. A rival group reanalyzed the data to suggest a younger date of 47 kyr, which they acknowledged still implicated Neanderthals – although, in the one place where a putatively Neanderthal abstract design (rather than color splotch or hand stencil) was given a very early date, the lines in question appeared to be part of a larger assemblage in which other dates came in at around 12 kyr. Since there is nothing comparable elsewhere in the Neanderthal record, many thus prefer to suspend judgment until a little more evidence for Neanderthal cave decoration, or other overtly symbolic activity, comes in. Meanwhile, we are left with a host of hints that are individually suggestive about Neanderthal cognitive complexity, but that are basically floating points, bereft of a larger context in which to place them. Currently, it seems most reasonable to conclude that, while a bright Neanderthal occasionally did something intriguing that anticipated what a fully symbolic human might do, such expressions were not a routine part of the Neanderthal behavioral repertoire. The Neanderthals existed for a long time, over a vast swath of Eurasia, and they are well documented at many sites. If symbolic reasoning had been a regular property of the species, we would surely have more evidence of it than those few straws in the wind – especially given that, in the short time it has been symbolic, *Homo sapiens* has radically altered the face of our planet.

One question everyone asks is, "did Neanderthals have language?" To which, the answer almost certainly is "no." That is emphatically not to suggest that the Neanderthals lacked sophisticated verbal communication that would have been supplemented, as in our own case, by elaborate gestural and postural expression. But verbal communication is not synonymous with spoken language, which is a particular way of structuring communication so that an endless variety of specific meanings can be conjured from a handful of basic elements. Language in this sense maps perfectly on to symbolic thought, as we will explore further in the next chapter; and if you do not reason symbolically, it is vanishingly improbable that you will have language (and vice-versa). So, while Neanderthal verbal communication was doubtless highly sophisticated, it was almost certainly not language. Just for the record, reconstructions of Neanderthal vocal tracts tend to suggest that these hominins were not capable of producing the full range of formant frequencies that are needed to speak as all languages are spoken today. And while Neanderthal possession of language has recently been inferred from studies suggesting that their hearing apparatus could detect the full range of frequencies we use to produce language today, it is important to bear in mind that while an adequate hearing system may be a necessary condition for language, it is not a sufficient one.

All in all, then, *Homo neanderthalensis* emerges as a tough, capable, flexible, and in many ways admirable species that was in its time as smart and manually skillful as any hominin had ever been. It shows us, above all, that there are ways other than our own to be an intelligent hominin. Neanderthals had a keen intuitive understanding of their many environments, which they exploited with subtlety and insight. They were capable of strong personal attachment, as witnessed by the care they extended to handicapped individuals – although such instances as the El Sidrón massacre give us a glimpse of another side of the Neanderthal psyche entirely. Survivable injuries likely due to intragroup violence are known, but they do not occur at undue frequency, suggesting that Neanderthal societies were effectively regulated by means other than coercion. The Neanderthals also had an aesthetic sense, and they may well have been just as moved by the beauty of a color-streaked sunset as any of us is today. And although we have no way to access how individual Neanderthals interacted in their daily lives, those interactions were evidently not so vastly different from our own as to have made it impossible to establish social relations, at some level, with the ungrateful *H. sapiens* who interbred with them before ousting them from their territory. There was, in other words, a huge amount of us in them – and vice-versa.

What the Neanderthals were not, however, was symbolic. Whether they had the underlying potential to become symbolic is something we will likely never know: A handful of short-lived and often disputed cultures that developed in Europe just before their disappearance combine both Neanderthal and Upper Paleolithic forms of expression, but don't help us to answer this question. Still, whatever the case, as sensitively as they may have reacted to the world around them, the nonsymbolic Neanderthals still lived in that world as they found it. They existed on the other side of the symbolic cognitive gulf that only *Homo sapiens* has ever contrived to cross – likely at the expense of a price paid in quality of experience that only increasing knowledge of the Neanderthals will help us eventually understand.

8 The Emergence and Spread of *Homo sapiens*

Origin of *Homo sapiens* in Africa

There is little, if anything, in the hominin fossil record that can be said to closely anticipate the very derived anatomy of our species *Homo sapiens*. Compared to other members of the genus *Homo*, modern humans are exceptionally slenderly built, with narrow hips and barrel-shaped rib cages that taper both at the top and the bottom. Our skulls are high, short, and rounded (Figure 8.1); and instead of projecting, our very small faces are retracted beneath the front of our braincases. Our brow ridges vary from modestly protrusive to barely detectable, but they are invariably bipartite, with central and lateral surfaces separated by an oblique furrow. We are also alone among the hominins in having a true chin at the front of the lower jaw. This takes the form of an inverted "T," with a vertical ridge in the midline of the jaw atop a horizontal bar running between a pronounced tubercle on each side.

The comparison in Figure 8.2 between a Neanderthal and a modern human skeleton shows just how dramatic the anatomical contrast is between these two big-brained forms. In an extremely general sense, *H. sapiens* is usually considered to have emerged from *H. heidelbergensis*, which is represented in Africa in the 600- to 300-kyr range. And, while all known *heidelbergensis* individuals appear a bit too derived to have filled a direct ancestral role, it is possible that a population of the species somewhere in Africa, the continent in which *H. sapiens* first showed up, might have been less morphologically specialized. If *heidelbergensis* was not in some sense the ancestor, then exactly how our species emerged remains as yet undocumented by fossils.

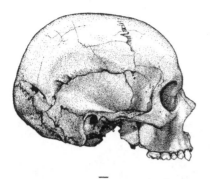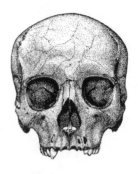

Figure 8.1　A representative modern human cranium, from El Hesa in Egypt. Scale is 1 cm.

In the period following around 400 to 300 kyr, an assortment of fossil hominins is known that were once grouped under the rubric of "archaic *Homo sapiens*." Use of this term is thankfully fading; the fossils in question are mainly united only by having biggish brains, and paleoanthropologists of linear mindset used it basically because they didn't know what else to do with them. African specimens in this category include crania found at Ngaloba/Laetoli (120 kyr, 1,367 ml, Figure 8.3, right) and Lake Ndutu (400 kyr, 1,280 ml, Figure 8.3, center) in Tanzania, Eliye Springs (300 to 200 kyr, 1,300–1,450 ml) in Kenya's West Turkana, and Florisbad in South Africa (260 kyr, ~1,400 ml). They also include a curious group of fossil hominins from the Mediterranean coast of Africa, among them the skull and partial skeleton of a child from the Contrebandiers Cave in northeastern Morocco (108 kyr), and two crania, a partial lower jaw, and a hip bone from Jebel Irhoud in that country's southwest (~300 kyr, 1,304 and 1,400 ml). The Maghreb materials, especially, beg to be revisited; but, pending that, it is most important to note than *none* of the African fossils just mentioned is justifiably placed in *Homo sapiens*, even though the Jebel Irhoud date is widely cited in support of the claim that anatomically modern *H. sapiens* was already out and about by 300 kyr ago. The same can be said of fossils from sites in the Levant such as Mount Carmel's Es Skhūl and Jebel Qafzeh near Nazareth. Both localities are dated to over 100 kyr; Skhūl has produced

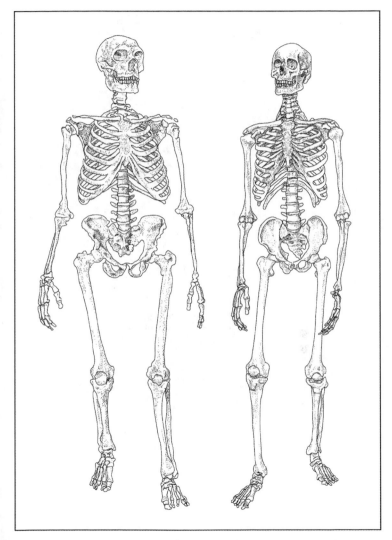

Figure 8.2 Comparison between the skeletons of a *Homo sapiens* (left), and a *Homo neanderthalensis* (right) of approximately equal stature.

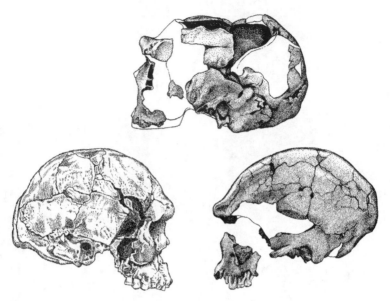

Figure 8.3 Three African Mid to Late Pleistocene crania. Left, the *Homo sapiens* "idaltu" cranium from Herto, Ethiopia; and center and right, respectively, the Lake Ndutu and Ngaloba/Laetoli crania that were often viewed as "archaic *Homo sapiens.*" Not to scale.

a series of crania that are certainly not the modern *Homo sapiens* they are often alleged to be, while Qafzeh has yielded both *Homo sapiens* individuals and others that look considerably more archaic. Since Neanderthals were also in the Levant at the time, it is just conceivable that the odder-looking Skhūl and Qafzeh individuals might have been hybrids, a possibility that will only be testable when a DNA-verifiable hybrid of a similar kind is found.

The Levant thus remains a bit of a mystery; but since Neanderthals survived there until about 45 kyr ago, it is possible to guess that an early (pre-100 kyr) *Homo sapiens* foray into the region was only partly successful at best, the Levantine Neanderthals having been finally dislodged only by a much later modern incursion. In contrast, the African fossils just mentioned hold an important message: The long-established tendency of the genus *Homo* not only to diversify and explore its evolutionary potential, but to develop ever-larger brains, was still actively expressing itself in Africa until very close to the present. The anatomically recognizable species *Homo sapiens* presumably emerged from one of those many evolutionary experiments.

The best evidence for the early presence on our planet of fully anatomically modern humans comes from sites in Ethiopia. The oldest such intimation, now dated to as much as 233 kyr, is a fragmentary skull discovered by Richard Leakey's short-lived expedition to the Omo Basin of southern Ethiopia in 1967. As reconstructed, this specimen bears the major hallmarks of *Homo sapiens*. Most notably, its face is retracted, although it bears only a hint of a true chin. The braincase is too fragmentary to yield a volume, but a more archaic-looking skullcap found nearby came in at a hefty 1,491 ml. Some stone tools probably from the same horizon have been described as "unremarkable" and "generic" examples of the African Middle Stone Age (MSA), the local counterpart of the Neanderthals' Mousterian technology in Europe. Somewhat younger, but more complete, is an adult cranium from Herto, in Ethiopia's Middle Awash region (160 kyr, 1,450 ml, Figure 8.3, left). This was given its own subspecies name, *H. sapiens idaltu*; but subspecies are better avoided among hominin fossils, and the cranium's most important quality is that it clearly fits the *H. sapiens* rubric. It is associated with skull fragments of some other individuals of similar aspect, and a partial juvenile cranium. Lithics found nearby are of both Mode 3 and Mode 2 types, including some of the very last handaxes made in Africa. The Mode 3 tools were, again, "generic" for the early African MSA. Both the adult and the juvenile crania are reported to have been defleshed, and the juvenile was said to bear a "polish" that might have been acquired from transportation in a bag.

Between them, the Omo and Herto occurrences are good physical evidence that anatomically recognizable *Homo sapiens* was already around in the period following 200 kyr ago (intriguingly, members of a small group of large-brained and recent South African crania that includes fossils from Fish Hoek [<8 kyr, 1,400 ml], Boskop ["late Pleistocene," 1,800 ml], and Border Cave [~70 kyr, 1,510 ml] have all the hallmarks of the *H. sapiens* skull – except for the bipartite brow and the classic chin). The >200 kyr date for the first *H. sapiens* fossil meshes neatly with molecular studies that also converge on an origin of our species around this time. A 2019 mtDNA study, for example, suggested that the ancestral *H. sapiens* population lived in northern Botswana some 200 kyr ago, and that it began to move out of the area some 70 kyr later due to environmental changes. This is certainly not the last word on the subject, but it is part of an accumulating genomic literature that comfortingly agrees on the timing, if not on the exact location, of modern human emergence.

What should not surprise us, given the general lack of correspondence between the appearance of new hominins and new technologies, is the conservative nature of the stone tools produced by the newly minted *Homo sapiens*. We could certainly wish for a better archaeological record in this respect; but to the extent that behavior in the larger sense is reflected in technology, very early *H. sapiens* seem to have been behaving in much the same way as their own African predecessors and their contemporaries in Africa and elsewhere in the world. Members of the new species looked radically different from their closest relatives, but there is little suggestion that their visible distinctiveness corresponded with anything new in their lives.

Given both the suddenness of the arrival of the new species, and its physical distinctness from other known hominins of the period, the most parsimonious conclusion must be that, prior to or during the event of isolation and speciation that established our species, the genetic innovation that underwrote the new body form appeared spontaneously in a local African population that was small enough to allow its rapid incorporation into the local gene pool. And such populations are, in fact, exactly what one might expect for a recently evolved predator that was spread very thinly over the vast African landscape: a landscape that was, moreover, subject to abrupt environmental change as climates shifted on short timescales. Indeed, even today the immense population of *H. sapiens* shows a remarkably low level of genetic variability that has led genomics researchers to suggest that, at a time close to its origin, the species passed through a severe population bottleneck (for which, read "crash"), most likely due to severity of climate. The identity of the genomic change that was acquired at the time, and that wrought such far-reaching effects on the human frame and cognitive system, remains elusive. Most likely, though, it was an alteration that involved gene regulation rather than the protein-coding genes themselves.

Symbolic Behaviors

After anatomical *Homo sapiens* had been in existence for over 100 kyr, we begin to detect an inflection in the MSA archaeological record in Africa. Stone-tool making techniques remained basically the same (although local variants tended to proliferate in a much more pronounced fashion than we see in the Mousterian), but new things began to creep in alongside them. At about 100 kyr, Blombos Cave near the continent's southern tip hosted an "ochre-processing workshop" in which ground ochre was mixed with carriers and extenders into a complex liquid pigment that was stored in abalone shells. From around the same date, sites in Mediterranean and southern Africa and the Levant (including Skhūl) have produced deliberately pierced marine snail shells that were evidently strung for jewelry, and some of which bear traces of ochre pigment possibly acquired through contact with a painted body. Bodily decoration is perhaps not the ideal proxy for symbolic behaviors, but this new activity is at the very least highly suggestive, and more conclusive indications of symbolic thinking, in the form of overtly symbolic objects, are not long to await.

In archaeological layers dating to about 80 to 75 kyr ago, besides an impressive number of pierced and colored tick shells, Blombos has produced fragments of ochre plaques (and one complete one: see Figure 8.4, bottom) that were smoothed to a flat surface. That surface was then engraved with a hatched design that was clearly intentional, and that seems to have had a specific significance that was retained over time. These are the first overtly symbolic expressions we know of; and because they are not only accompanied by other apparently symbolic manifest-ations, but also herald a continuing practice of symbolic object produc-tion, we are on reasonably firm ground in concluding that by about 100 kyr ago hominids of the African MSA tradition had begun to process information in the modern symbolic manner. At the 73 kyr level in Blombos we find striking confirmation of this in the form of the earliest drawing known (Figure 8.4, top): another zig-zag abstract design, made this time by using an ochre crayon on a piece of silcrete (a hard rocky material made of silica-cemented soils and sands) with a naturally flat surface. Burial was evidently not practiced at this time, and we have

Figure 8.4   Top: the world's earliest drawing, from South Africa's Blombos Cave. Bottom: the most complete of the engraved plaques, from the same site, that are the earliest explicitly symbolic artifacts currently known. Not to exact scale.

a limited fossil record of the MSA people themselves; but the record we do have indicates that these complex expressions in the MSA were the work of anatomically modern humans.

Together with symbolic artifacts like these, significant advances were also being made in practical technologies. One of these, since then also observed at Blombos, was first identified a little farther east along the South African coast in one of the caves of the Pinnacle Point complex. There, certainly beginning by 72 kyr and likely much longer ago, MSA people were fire-hardening silcrete (which in its raw form readily flakes, but doesn't hold an edge) to turn it into an excellent material for stone tools. The process involved is long and complex, and it has been argued that it demanded symbolic planning. The same has also been claimed for the Pinnacle Point peoples' shell-fishing activities, which, it is said, would have required them to predict the tides along the coastline even as they moved widely across the landscape in search of sustenance.

Blombos and Pinnacle Point are not the only sites in South Africa to yield early evidence of symbolic behaviors; and an intriguing discovery at Sibudu Cave, on the country's east coast, was that of a 61-kyr-old bone needle, the first intimation we have of couture, another innovation that was made in Africa some tens of thousands of years before it appears in Europe. Following Sibudu times the African climate underwent a period of severe aridification, and the continent's southern tip became depopulated by humans. But by this point symbolic *Homo sapiens* had already begun to move out of the continent and into other areas of the Old World where (unlike their nonsymbolic predecessors who had forayed unsuccessfully into the Levant), they rapidly displaced all the resident hominid competition, from *Homo erectus* in the Far East to *H. neanderthalensis* in western Eurasia. Those who remained behind were evidently equally unkind to their remaining nonsymbolic African competitors as well.

The émigrés took with them their new way of relating to the world; and their most dramatic symbolic expression, and possibly the greatest of all time, was the extraordinary tradition of geometric and representative cave art that began in Europe at around 40 kyr ago, and lasted for an astonishing 30 kyr even as different waves of people came and went. Such sites as Lascaux, Font de Gaume, and Chauvet in France, and Altamira and Covalanas in Spain, contain some of the most powerful yet graceful figurative art that has ever been created (Figure 8.5). Although we still know nothing about the exact motivations of the hunter-gatherers who produced it, that art was clearly loaded with the deepest symbolic significance. Indeed, the representational art was routinely accompanied by geometric symbols that are sometimes repeated at different sites, suggesting a standardized regional significance. All in all, as alien to ours as their lifestyles and cosmologies might have been, there can be no doubt whatsoever that those Ice Age artists were both in skill and in intellectual capacity the equals of anyone in our modern postindustrial society. What is more, their displays of artistic virtuosity were accompanied, from the very beginning, not only by abundant evidence of unprecedentedly sophisticated levels of social and economic organization, but by such expressions as musical instruments, plaques bearing notations, and some of the most delicate and beautiful carvings and engravings ever made. All these manifestations in some way involved their makers' desire to understand the world around them,

Figure 8.5   Black-and-white rendering of a now badly faded Upper Paleolithic (Magdalenian) polychrome image of two reindeer, from the cave of Font de Gaume, in western France. A female kneels before a large male, who is leaning forward and tenderly licking her brow. Undated, but likely about 14 kyr old.

and to explain their place in it, making it clear that in their broadest senses both the artistic and the spiritual were baked into the human spirit from the very beginning. For this reason and many more, a pilgrimage to some of the cave art sites in France and Spain should be on the bucket list of anyone, from anywhere, who cares about where he or she came from.

And maybe Indonesia should be on that list, too. In 2014 the world was amazed by a report that an image of a babirusa (a local pig relative) in a limestone cave on the island of Sulawesi had been dated, by uranium-series on overlying calcite, to about 35 kyr. Some nearby handprints came in even earlier, at about 40 kyr old. At the time, this was as old as any cave markings yet dated in Europe; but in 2018 it was dramatically upstaged by a 40 kyr date for images of cow-like creatures on a cave wall in the neighboring island of Borneo. The same cave also contained black handprints that might have been as much as 50 kyr old. Sulawesi snatched back the laurels for the world's oldest representational painting the next year, when a panel decorated with a buffalo, wild pigs, and some smaller anthropomorphs (with tails and snouts) came in at around 44 kyr. If a single design (not a sure bet), this panel would be distinguished from the vast bulk of European cave art, in which narrative scenes seem to have been almost completely avoided.

With early representational art now documented in both Asia and Europe from the period around 40 kyr ago, it is natural to inquire whether the two phenomena were independent local developments, or whether they might have had a common source. There is no way to be sure about this, but a best guess is that both stemmed from a single tradition that most plausibly originated in Africa, prior to the exodus of fully symbolic modern humans. Since both molecular and paleontological sources of evidence suggest that this exodus was underway by 70 to 55 kyr ago, the inference must be that representational art began in Africa not long after we find the first stirrings there of the symbolic spirit – despite a dearth of direct evidence that is most likely due to the continent's huge size and its under-exploration by archaeologists. And if that is the case, then the transition from a nonsymbolic human condition to a fully-fledged symbolic one came about breathtakingly fast.

In the Beginning Was the Word

How can we explain this amazing transition? Well, we need to start with the recognition that no new way of doing things can be introduced until the necessary biology is there. You simply cannot function in a new way if you don't have the potential to do it. Accordingly, the structures and capacities underwriting symbolic cognition must already have been in place when humans began to behave in the radically new fashion. And the only obvious event in which that capacity might have been acquired was the one, perhaps around 250 kyr ago, in which humans acquired their striking new anatomical specializations. We know that this developmental change had profound resonances, throughout the body, in the hard tissues which are all that preserve in the fossil record; and there is no reason to believe that this same change should not have had repercussions in the nonpreserving soft tissues as well, and specifically in the brain. The exact neural innovations involved are beyond our remit here, but they will certainly have included improved signal pathways between different parts of the brain. And as far as we can tell from the archaeological record, the resulting enhanced potential for making mental associations lay unused for a short but significant period, during which members of *Homo sapiens* continued to behave much as their predecessors had done. But then the new potential was recruited, by what was necessarily a cultural or behavioral stimulus. In evolutionary terms this would not have been at all unusual: the predecessors of birds, for example, had possessed feathers for many millions of years before co-opting them as essential adjuncts to flight. Similarly, the ancestors of the first land-living tetrapods acquired their bone-reinforced limbs while still swimming in the seas.

So, what was the behavioral stimulus that kicked a preadapted brain into working on a symbolic algorithm? Well, paleoanthropologists of sociobiological bent have long looked to the complexities of modern social behaviors. We are higher primates, the most intensely social members of an intensely social taxon; and we are able to read the minds of others in unusually subtle and detached ways that, some believe, were driven into existence by the dynamics of interaction among individuals in societies that were steadily becoming more complex. However, such explanations not only pose such unanswerable questions as why the members of only one higher primate lineage became symbolic, but also describe a very gradual process that would have taken vast amounts of time to unfurl to the extent we see in modern *Homo sapiens*. If, indeed, such a transition would even have been possible, given that mechanisms of this kind do nothing to address the qualitative difference between two ways of thinking that do not exist on the same continuum. The stimulus we are seeking not only acted extremely rapidly, but also involved a radical shift in cognitive function. And a much better candidate for that stimulus is the spontaneous invention of language.

What makes language the best – if not the only – possibility in this context is that language maps perfectly onto symbolic thought. Like thought, language depends on a vocabulary of discrete symbols that can be combined and recombined, according to rules, to make statements not only about the world as we perceive it, but as it *might* be. And it is, indeed, virtually impossible for us to conceive of thought in the absence of language. We modern humans make all kinds of intuitive associations in our brains, it is true; but to explain them to ourselves as well as to others requires the intermediation of language. The many cultural achievements of other hominins show clearly that very complex behaviors may be generated intuitively, without the benefit of language; but behavior in the peculiarly modern human symbolic manner is, like our ability to reimagine the world, entirely language dependent. And there is good reason from linguistics as well as from archaeology and genomics to believe that language began in Africa, where the first intimations of symbolism are found. That's because language itself evolves, and very quickly: Beyond about 5–10 kyr it is impossible to trace the descent of languages from internal and comparative evidence. But the basic sounds – the phonemes – from which verbal language is made tend to linger; and several years ago a study found that the farther away from Africa you go, the fewer phonemes there are. This is just what you would expect if Africa had been the center of language origin, and phonemes elsewhere had been subsequently lost due to the drop in effective population sizes as mobile descendant groups budded off from their ancestors.

If the invention of language was the stimulus, the rapidity of the transition from nonsymbolic to symbolic cognition is easily explained. All modern humans live in societies with established vocal languages; but deaf people with all the neural equipment of hearing ones also need to communicate, and they do this by using sign languages that are every bit as intricate and rulebound as their verbal counterparts. And, in one famous instance, linguistics researchers were able to witness a sign language being spontaneously invented, by deaf Nicaraguan children who had been brought up isolated in hearing households, but had finally been brought together in a boarding school. With no previous experience of signing, they spontaneously and almost immediately devised a rule-driven sign language that was rapidly refined as the generations of schoolkids turned over. This analogy for the invention and transmission of spoken language is even more attractive for being the achievement of children, because adults (even ones with predisposed brains) are usually reluctant (or even unable) to do things in new ways, as a classic Japanese study of macaques showed. To attract the monkeys to a beach where they could be studied, researchers strewed sweet potatoes on the sand. These tasty items became unpleasantly gritty, and some young macaques spontaneously started to wash off the sand in the sea. This habit quickly spread to lower-ranking adult females, and then up through the hierarchy, although some of the crustiest dominant males never adopted it at all.

In trying to envisage the emergence of language, one can easily imagine a small, isolated encampment of early *Homo sapiens*, somewhere in Africa, where playing children started to attach specific meanings – most likely initially object names – to sounds that they had already learned as part of an existing vocal repertoire. This would have created a feedback in their minds between sound and meaning, and it could have led to structured language in a fashion very similar to what the linguists observed in Nicaragua. The key here was a brain already structured to make the mental associations involved; and since all early anatomical *Homo sapiens* would already have possessed such a brain, the new way of communicating could rapidly have spread upward within the immediate group and then beyond, taking complexifying symbolic thought along with it as the vocabulary grew and the rules were refined. An influential school of linguistics holds that both language and thought depend on a very simple basic mental operation, making this scenario even more plausible – as mind-boggling as it may be, even in principle, to imagine that shift from the nonsymbolic to the symbolic algorithm, maybe the most radical cognitive change ever.

Incredibly, it is possible that someone has actually witnessed such a shift taking place. In her book *A Man Without Words*, the sign-language teacher Susan Schaller writes of realizing that one of her deaf students not only lacked knowledge of how to sign, but also had no idea that other people used names to denote objects. This made it difficult to get across the significance of signs to him; but once Schaller managed it, her student, whom she called Ildefonso, went through an epiphany as he realized that things had names: "Suddenly he sat up straight and rigid ... the whites of his eyes expanded, as if in terror." This was a hugely emotional moment for him; but, after his sobs had subsided, he became hungry for names, and more names. Schaller writes very movingly of the sense of grief that overcame him as he perceived how he had "existed alone, shut out of the human race." Still, the story ended reasonably happily because Ildefonso eventually mastered American Sign Language – significantly, with all the difficulties that adults typically experience in learning a new language. But his struggles had helped Schaller to obtain an insight into his earlier "intelligent, sane, yet languageless" state. It later transpired that Ildefonso had belonged to a small community of individuals who shared his symbolic deficit and communicated by miming. In "conversing" with one another they acted out their experiences, a practice that was so inefficient and time-consuming that, once linguistic, the exasperated Ildefonso lost patience and ceased associating with his former friends. Sadly, he also refused to use his mastery of sign language to discuss his previous quality of life; apparently, the recollection was just too traumatic.

The notion that the human brain underwent a recent and sudden algorithmic shift, a radical change in the way in which it worked, is supported by the rather counterintuitive fact that, after two million years of steady expansion, our brains apparently shrank significantly following the end of the last Ice Age. Both the Neanderthals and the early modern Europeans who replaced them seem to have had brains of approximately equal volume (averaging about 1,500 ml), making both some 13 percent bigger than the brains of people today (ca. 1,330 ml). Especially because brain tissue is metabolically so costly, this shrinkage supports the suggestion that the ancestral "intuitive" hominid brain operated on a "brute-force" algorithm in which "intelligence," however you might wish to define it, scaled up more or less directly with brain volume. In contrast, the new symbolic algorithm turned out to be a much more metabolically frugal one, demanding less energy input to produce a distinctively different cognitive product. As accidental as it might have been, the energy-efficient new symbolic cognitive style turned out to generate a product that was not only emergently different, but that also made its possessors significantly more effective in the competition for ecological space than any other hominin that had previously existed. So effective, indeed, that for the first time ever the early symbolic humans rapidly cleared out the competition, and bequeathed us our unprecedented status as the world's only hominin.

Homo sapiens Takes Over the World

Symbolic *Homo sapiens* populations evidently expanded rapidly within Africa, and molecular estimates suggest that fully modern humans had begun to spread beyond their natal continent in the period between about 70 and 55 kyr ago. What happened thereafter is to some extent documented by the morphology of fossil finds; but it is better calibrated by DNA comparisons among living populations, and by ancient DNA (aDNA) extracted from early *Homo sapiens* fossils. The latter provide crucial data because, for example, some historically important DNA lineages have been lost, meaning that we can only know about them from fossil sources. Others survive only as genomic fragments, to which fossils can help put a face (and a more complete genome). The favorite method of reconstructing ancient migrations traditionally involved tracing the spread and diversification of mtDNA and Y chromosome haplogroups, but nuclear DNA is increasingly being analyzed in this context too. In terms of geography, there seem to have been two migration routes out of Africa. One was up the Nile valley and thence overland across the Sinai into the Levant and onward, while the other led from today's Djibouti, across the narrow (but fast-moving) Bab El Mandab strait, and into southern Yemen. This was a less forbidding route than it might seem because, at least periodically, Arabia was not the sandy waste it is today.

Eastern Africans of the L_3 mitochondrial haplogroup seem to have been involved in an episode of intermittent emigration that is substantiated in western Eurasia by the L_3-derived M and N haplogroups and their derivatives. Those migrants followed the (now largely drowned) southern coastline of Asia eastward, ultimately finding their way into the islands of southeast Asia where they were already established over 45 kyr ago. One branch seems to have peeled off toward Europe, eventually even finding its way back into north Africa. A study in 2016 of 55 complete genomes of ancient European hunter-gatherers revealed that, in the remote past, the M haplotype had been present in Europe as well as elsewhere in Eurasia. This strongly suggested that all the major non-African haplotypes had resulted from a single rapid dispersal out of Africa at around 55 kyr ago. That date fit quite well with the estimate for hybridization with Denisovans by eastbound modern humans at about 54 to 44 kyr, and it overlaps with the current Neanderthal hybridization estimate, at 65 to 47 kyr. The Denisovan contribution to modern populations is highest in New Guinea and neighboring islands, and one Denisovan allele seems eventually to have facilitated the human occupation of the Tibetan highlands by about 40 to 30 kyr. It should be noted that, although "Neanderthal genes" have now been reported in Africa as well as in Eurasia, they are attributed to back-migrations within the last several thousand years.

Early migrants out of tropical Africa seem to have turned eastward, staying in relatively balmy climes; but by around 45 kyr ago populations ultimately of African origin had begun to trickle into chilly Europe in significant numbers (and, by around 30 kyr ago, they were already north of the Arctic Circle). A 2016 molecular study of over 50 European skeletons dating between 45 and 7 kyr ago showed that over this relatively brief period the proportion of Neanderthal DNA in the European genome decreased from as much as 3–6 percent to around 2 percent, suggesting that in the interim there had been strong natural selection against the Neanderthal genes and phenotypes that had been acquired by interbreeding not long before.

The very earliest modern Europeans seem to have made little if any specific genomic contribution to the people living in the peninsula today; and individuals sampled in the later 37- to 14-kyr range, from Spain in the west to Russia in the east, all seem to have been descended from a single founder population that somehow left no genomic traces in modern Europeans. Within this larger pattern, several time-constrained genomic population "clusters" have been identified. In the western part of this vast area, these clusters appeared to correspond to the Gravettian (sampled between 34 and 26 kyr) and Magdalenian (19 to 14 kyr) Paleolithic cultures, and to the post-Paleolithic (14 to 7 kyr) Azilian and Mesolithic ones. A genomic feature that had been associated with the earlier Aurignacians, but that was absent among the Gravettians, also resurfaced at around 19 kyr, suggesting to researchers that the Aurignacians who had originally entered Europe had been marginalized by the Gravettians into a refugium – possibly Iberia – from which they were finally able to re-emerge when the climate cooled again. The post-Paleolithic population clusters showed significant Near Eastern influences, suggesting a major population influx from this source as the climate warmed following the Last Glacial Maximum. And then, at about 4.4 kyr ago, there was another major population turnover in Europe, as the warlike and patriarchal equestrian peoples known to us as the Yamnaya flooded in from the central Eurasian steppes. This invasion would have been an enormously traumatic event for the quasi-sedentary resident Europeans; and it seems likely that, at least in part, they were so completely replaced because the newcomers brought with them the plague, a disease against which they were immunologically defenseless. The steppe people also introduced the ancestral Indo-European language, from which almost all languages spoken in Europe today are descended.

In agreement with some molecular estimates, the fossil record offers no certain indications that *Homo sapiens* had arrived in eastern Asia before about 55 to 50 kyr ago. The A, B, and G haplotypes seem to have differentiated in eastern Asia by about 50 kyr ago, and populations bearing these variants subsequently colonized Siberia, Korea, and Japan. After leaving Africa, the coastline-following émigrés had discovered India early on; and, to put it very crudely, today's very diverse Indian population seems to be largely derived from the intermixing of a southern influence from this very early source, and a northern one ultimately drawn from the same steppic peoples as those who brought the Indo-European languages to Europe. Interestingly, while the mtDNA of Indians tends to be pretty solidly subcontinental, the Y chromosome data converge on a single ancestral genotype from very roughly 6,000 years ago, suggesting that the northern genomic signal may have come from male-dominated invading armies. If so, this would be an example of the "Genghis Khan" phenomenon: Today, some 16 million men ultimately of Central Asian origin carry a Y chromosome variant believed to have originated with the famed twelfth-century Mongolian conqueror.

In general, the genomic makeups of most of today's Asian populations seem to be largely due to relatively recent events, as expansions of agricultural peoples in Asia, often at the expense of resident hunter-gatherers, obliterated traces of a greater past diversity. Thus, a 2019 study found that agricultural populations that differentiated around 10 kyr ago in the valleys of the Yellow, Yangtze, and Pearl Rivers began to coalesce into today's Han Chinese only in the last few thousand years. In Australia, in contrast, analysis of a 100-year-old aboriginal hair sample concluded that the genome represented was descended from an early human dispersal into eastern Asia that preceded the one that gave rise to most of today's East Asian populations. Those early explorers had exchanged genes with the Denisovans on the way east, before reaching Australia (across a 50-mile ocean gap) by about 50 kyr ago. In one of the last major human population expansions, the islands of Oceania were colonized beginning at about 5.5 kyr by seafaring humans who were resident in Taiwan, but whose roots lay earlier, somewhere in mainland East Asia.

The Americas were the last of the habitable continents to be occupied by *Homo sapiens*; and although the genomic picture is still very incomplete due partly to a dearth of ancient North American individuals available for study, it seems that the colonization was a more complicated business than archaeologists had thought. There is no doubt, though, that the first Americans originated in Siberia, crossing into North America over a land bridge across the Bering Strait that was exposed between about 30 and 12 kyr ago, or crossing in boats and following a coastal route down the western seaboard. Some Late Pleistocene population mixing in Siberia evidently gave rise to two lineages, one ancestral to the Chukchi and other modern Siberian groups, and the other to a "basal American branch." That split must have occurred before 21 to 20 kyr ago, which is when the basal branch began itself splitting into several exclusively New World lineages. An "ancient Beringian" lineage apparently went extinct, while an "ancestral Native American" lineage continued south to bud off a terminal lineage at around 21 to 16 kyr, and then to split at around 15.7 kyr into "Native North American" and "Native South American" lineages, the latter rapidly dispersing into South America, where further splits occurred. The migrant populations would have been very small, and there were doubtless a lot of minor lineage divisions and local extinctions along the way, especially as this was a time of extreme climatic fluctuation. The genomic timescale is broadly consistent with generally agreed archaeological dates, but there is nonetheless a steady drumbeat of discoveries suggesting significantly earlier human occupation of the New World by people who left no recognized genomic traces. The latest entrant in the "oldest New World site" stakes is Mexico's high-altitude Chiquihuite Cave, which has yielded a trove of stone tools claimed to date between 25 and 32 kyr ago. Inevitably, this claim is disputed (the flakes are not actually tools; over the years they had shifted in the deposits), but there will be more such cases (like the 22.8-kyr-old human footprints from White Sands, New Mexico, that were announced after this book went to press), and only time will tell.

Epilogue

The message from the population movements briefly recounted in the previous chapter is that *Homo sapiens* has been an itinerant species from the outset. Even in a world with intensively patrolled political borders there is no reason to believe that this propensity will be contained any time soon: It is an ongoing phenomenon that will have to be managed, hopefully as humanely as possible. More generally, the message deriving from the story told in this book is that we modern human beings have an astonishingly recent origin, and a sudden one. In evolutionary terms, we acquired our extraordinary symbolic reasoning capacities virtually overnight, and we did so exaptively (i.e., not in the context familiar today) rather than *ada*ptively (within that symbolic context). What this most importantly tells us is that we cannot have been fine-tuned by natural selection over the eons to be the kind of creature we are today; there was simply not enough time. Which in turn suggests that, within the limits of circumstance, Nature has (albeit unintentionally) given human beings almost unlimited freedom to become the kinds of creatures they individually choose to be. We can only express this freedom, however, by using some rather jury-rigged cognitive equipment that was most certainly not optimized by evolution to respond to the demands we routinely place upon it. We are, for instance, terrible judges of risk. We have very malleable memory systems. We allow our emotions to interfere with our rational judgments, we believe (seriously) weird things, and we congratulate ourselves on being things that we are not. When I was once challenged to come up with a true "human universal," the best I could come up with was the rather unflattering "cognitive dissonance." That thought has rather dismal resonances for the vaunted "human condition" over which so much ink has been spilled across the centuries; and indeed, you could argue that the human condition does not in fact exist, at least in the sense of being definable. After all, simply being a member of *Homo sapiens* predicts remarkably little about the qualities of any individual, other than that they are a featherless biped.

It remains true, of course, that the most remarkable feature of humankind (and perhaps our only true "human universal") is our capacity to remake the world in our heads. But even this is hardly an unalloyed blessing, because while this ability is undeniably the fount of our creativity, it also makes it possible for us to imagine that things *could* be better than they are or than we can make them, which often leads to chronic states of existential dissatisfaction. Nonetheless, in our imperfect human world, most of us find our cognitive deficiencies to be a perfectly acceptable price to pay for the enjoyment of the many hugely positive aspects of being human: the abilities, for example, to experience love, joy, insight, inspiration, and exhilaration. And it is certainly satisfying to be able to reject the notion that we are simply soulless rational automatons. On the flip side, however, the rather random and undirected nature of the process by which we got here means that we cannot, as some would have us believe, assuage our consciences by blaming our failings and bad decisions on hard-wired responses that were originally developed to deal with a now-vanished "environment of evolutionary adaptation." We are not the hapless victims of atavistic impulse: instead, we really do have choices, and we truly are individually responsible for what we do.

And one final thought. Another message of this book is that our lineage came a long way very quickly. And with such a head of steam behind us, might we not expect that future evolution will eventually fix our defects? Well, probably not. One of the reasons why our lineage saw so much change accumulate so quickly is that our hunting-gathering Pleistocene predecessors lived in very small populations that were very thinly spread over vast landscapes. These were exactly the circumstances in which you would expect spontaneously arising genetic novelties to become rapidly and regularly fixed. What is more, Pleistocene climatic vicissitudes would frequently have isolated those tiny populations, setting the stage for the other main component of evolutionary change, speciation. But since the adoption of sedentary agriculture, right at the end of the Ice Ages, the human population has been on a steady trajectory of worldwide growth. There are now almost eight billion of us; and as individuals we are unprecedentedly mobile. Packed cheek-by-jowl across the continents, the human species is now a single huge interbreeding population within which the probability of incorporating significant genetic innovations is negligible. Gene frequencies will continue to slosh around, of course; but under current demographic circumstances it is highly unlikely that a new and improved version of humankind will emerge. Unless, of course, some all-too-easily imaginable disaster might fragment the human population, and thereby open the door once again to evolutionary change. But failing that unappetizing possibility, if we are going to get by on a planet that is already rebelling forcefully against our heedless exploitation of it, we shall have to learn to live responsibly with our unoptimized selves as we are. Fortunately, though, as one door closes another opens. The prospects for biological improvement may be remote; but we are still only at the beginning of our explorations of the capacity for cultural innovation that our unique symbolic abilities have conferred on us.

Summary of Common Misunderstandings

Evolution is "just" a theory. Science is not in search of eternal truths. It progresses by formulating hypotheses about how the world works, and then testing them against observations of that world, often experimental, to produce an increasingly accurate description of that world. A theory is an explanation that has survived repeated testing, and thus is the closest thing that science has to a fact. In the case of evolution, what Charles Darwin succinctly described as "descent with modification" has not only resisted repeated attempts to falsify it as the causative mechanism for the riotous diversity of the natural world, but also it is the only explanation we have that actually predicts the nested way in which that diversity is organized.

The human fossil record is pretty thin. Not at all. Paleoanthropologists regularly complain that they need more fossils to answer the questions that the last discovery raised – but then, if they didn't, who would give them grants to enable them to find more and keep the enterprise going? More fossils are, of course, always desirable; but over the past several decades the human fossil record has greatly expanded, to give us a pretty comprehensive picture of what transpired in human evolution over the past 7 myr or so. Still, while we are now at a point at which it is unlikely that any one new fossil discovery will require a complete redrawing of the human evolutionary picture, many specific questions remain.

Human evolution involved the fine-tuning of the human lineage, over vast periods of time, to its present point of perfection. Well, we can certainly argue about perfection; after all, our species is self-evidently a highly flawed bundle of contradictions. And it is also evident that the history of the hominin subfamily did not involve the gradual polishing of an evolving lineage by natural selection. We didn't simply climb a ladder. Instead, hominin history might metaphorically be perceived as one of vigorous experimentation: New species were repeatedly produced and tossed out into the ecological arena, to succeed or to become extinct in competition both with their close relatives and with other components of the biota.

Evolution optimizes. No. Natural selection is not like an engineer, trying to find the ideal solution to problems that arise. Most of the time it simply keeps populations fit by eliminating extremes. As a biped, for example, you are more likely to survive and reproduce successfully if you have two legs, rather than one, or three. Evolution is an untidy process that has to build however awkwardly upon what is there; and both as an individual and a species it is not necessary to be the best: Often, it is sufficient just to be good enough to get by. After all, if chased by a bear, you only need to be faster than the slowest member of your group; and a species in the evolutionary arena just needs to be better than the competition, whatever that might happen to be.

Evolutionary change is always adaptive. Evolutionary changes originate in spontaneous mutations of the DNA that occur simply as copying errors, without regard to any consequences they might have. Most of them will be problematic and will be eliminated. Of the rest, some may be neutral in effect, and will often hang around simply because they are not getting in the way of survival and reproduction. Sometimes circumstances may change to make such innovations useful and adaptive, as happened in the case of tetrapod limbs, which were acquired in the oceans long before being co-opted for terrestrial locomotion. Beneficial innovations may be useful right away, in which case they will be adaptive from the start, although it is important to remember that genetic changes usually have multiple effects, so that what succeeds or fails in nature is not particular character complexes, but rather the whole organism.

Human evolution involved the gradual transformation of an ancient ape ancestor into the modern species *Homo sapiens.* The ancient human ancestor was an ape in the broadest sense, but did not closely resemble any of today's great apes: We all have many million years of independent evolution. In terms of pattern, the story of human evolution was clearly not one of continuous transformation under the guiding hand of natural selection.

Innovation was instead episodic, as various human precursors were buffeted by the vicissitudes of Ice Age climates, with many extinctions along the way. Before the appearance of cognitively modern humans, cultural innovations were also sporadic and rare, with long periods of nonchange intervening between the introductions of new technologies.

The human ancestor was a knuckle-walker. When on the ground the gorillas and chimpanzees, our closest relatives, walk quadrupedally by folding their hands and taking the weight of their bodies on the proximal knuckles. This protects their long, slender grasping fingers when they are not needed to grasp branches, and it throws their body weight efficiently forward when on all fours. If we are more closely related to chimpanzees than to gorillas, it would seem logical to conclude that our own arboreal ancestor was a knuckle-walker too. But there is absolutely no fossil evidence that this was the case, and there is nothing in the structure of our hands to suggest a knuckle-walking ancestry.

The adoption of bipedality by ancient hominins occurred because it freed the hands to make tools. Freeing the hands from locomotion certainly made it possible to develop hands with a very precise grip. But tools only began to be made long after hominins had become upright. As a result, various other advantages to bipedality have been proposed, but the key thing to remember is that once you have stood up, all those potential advantages are yours. And all the disadvantages, too. The most important thing was standing up in the first place, probably because the ancestor was already most comfortable with suspending its body weight in the trees and therefore preferred to keep its trunk erect.

Bipedality first evolved on the open African savannas. Because bipedality involves walking and running, activities best carried out in the open, once early bipeds had been discovered in Africa it seemed natural to conclude that this unusual locomotion had evolved in that continent's vast open grasslands. However, further discoveries have shown that the first bipeds still depended on trees for shelter, and for some of their sustenance, favoring mixed habitats that ranged from forest edges to woodlands to bushlands and that rarely included truly open grassy environments. A true move into (and commitment to) the open only occurred after our own genus *Homo* had come along.

Large brains evolved very early in human evolution. Early paleoanthropologists often assumed that because large brains are the most vaunted feature of modern humans, they must also have characterized the first hominins. This was the fallacy that made possible the success of the Piltdown fraud in the early twentieth century. In fact, bipedality came long before the big brain.

Brain size correlates with intelligence. Leaving aside the fraught question of what "intelligence" is, it has become clear that over most of human evolution hominins were indulging in increasingly complex behaviors as average hominin brain sizes increased (though it is not clear exactly how this pattern played out: When we recognize an adequate number of extinct hominin species, we may realize that larger-brained species were outcompeting smaller-brained ones). In the end, however, once our own large-brained species had become symbolic and eliminated the competition, its average brain size promptly dropped. This suggests that how the brain is organized, and how it functions, are more important than raw brain size by itself in determining complexity of cognition.

Neanderthals were stupid and brutish. Hardly. These extinct human relatives had brains as large as those of contemporaneous *Homo sapiens*, and a huge repertoire of sophisticated behaviors. The chances are that they lacked the modern human symbolic cognitive capacity; but that certainly does not mean that they were dumb. They were clever, adroit, and resourceful, and they exploited their environments with great finesse. What they show us is that it is possible to be and do all these things in the absence of the symbolic style of intelligence that is the hallmark of *Homo sapiens*. Evidently, there are ways other than ours in which to be a very smart hominin.

References and Further Reading

The citations below include all journal articles and books to which direct reference is made in the text, plus others (marked with asterisks) that authoritatively survey the issues raised in the relevant chapters. Be guided by title.

General

DeSilva, J. (2021). *First Steps: How Upright Walking Made Us Human*. New York: Harper.

*Henke, W. and Tattersall, I. (eds) (2015). *Handbook of Paleoanthropology*, 3 vols, 2nd ed. Heidelberg: Springer.

*Klein, R. G. (2009). *The Human Career: Human Biological and Cultural Origins*, 3rd ed. Chicago: University of Chicago Press.

*Tattersall, I. (2012). *Masters of the Planet: The Search for Our Human Origins*. New York: Palgrave Macmillan.

*Tattersall, I. (2015). *The Strange Case of the Rickety Cossack and Other Cautionary Tales from Human Evolution*. New York: Palgrave Macmillan.

*Wood, B. A. (2019). *Human Evolution: A Very Short Introduction*, 2nd ed. Oxford: Oxford University Press.

Chapter 1

Darwin, C. (1859). *On the Origin of Species by Natural Selection, or The Preservation of Favoured Races in the Struggle for Life*. London: John Murray.

*DeSalle, R. and Tattersall, I. (2018). *Troublesome Science: The Misuse of Genetics and Genomics in Understanding Race*. New York: Columbia University Press.

Dobzhansky, T. (1937). *Genetics and the Origin of Species*. New York: Columbia University Press.

Dobzhansky, T. (1944). On species and races of living and fossil man. *American Journal of Physical Anthropology* 2: 251–265.

Eldredge, N. (1971). The allopatric model and phylogeny in Paleozoic vertebrates. *Evolution* 25: 156–167.

*Eldredge, N. (2015). *Eternal Ephemera: Adaptation and the Origin of Species from the Nineteenth Century Through Punctuated Equilibria and Beyond*. New York: Columbia University Press.

Eldredge, N. and Gould, S. J. (1972). Punctuated equilibria: An alternative to phyletic gradualism. In: T. J. M. Schopf (ed.), *Models in Paleobiology*, pp. 82–115. San Francisco: Freeman Cooper.

Fisher, R. A. (1918). The correlation between relatives on the supposition of Mendelian inheritance. *Transactions of the Royal Society of Edinburgh* 52: 399–433.

*Gould, S. J. (2002). *The Structure of Evolutionary Theory*. Cambridge, MA: Belknap Press.

Hennig, W. (1966). *Phylogenetic Systematics*. Urbana: University of Illinois Press.

*Kampourakis, K. (2020). *Understanding Evolution*. Cambridge: Cambridge University Press.

Lamarck, L. B. de. (1809). *Philosophie Zoologique*. Paris: Dentu.

Mayr, E. (1942). *Systematics and the Origin of Species, from the Viewpoint of a Zoologist*. Cambridge, MA: Harvard University Press.

*Mayr, E. (1982). *The Growth of Biological Thought*. Cambridge, MA: Belknap Press.

Mendel, J. G. (1866). *Versuche über Pflanzenhybriden. Verhandlungen des naturforschenden Vereines in Brünn*, Bd. IV für das Jahr, 1865, *Abhandlungen*: 3–47.

Nelson, G. (1979). Cladistic analysis and synthesis: Principles and definitions, with a historical note on Adanson's *Familles des Plantes* (1763–1764). *Systematic Zoology* 28: 2–29.

Tattersall, I. and Eldredge, N. (1977). Fact, theory, and fantasy in human paleontology. *American Scientist* 65: 204–211.

*Tattersall, I. (2010). *Paleontology: A Brief History of Life*. Conshohocken: Templeton Foundation Press.

Chapter 2

*Andel, T. H. van and Davies, W. (eds) (2003). *Neanderthals and Modern Humans in the European Landscape during the Last Glaciation*. Cambridge: McDonald Institute Monographs.

*Bradley, R. (2015). *Paleoclimatology: Reconstructing Climates of the Quaternary*. Oxford: Elsevier.

*Cohen, K. M. and Gibbard, P. L. (2011). *Global Chronostratigraphical Correlation Table for the Last 2.7 Million Years*. Cambridge: Subcommission on Quaternary Stratigraphy, International Commission on Stratigraphy.

*DeSalle, R. and Yudell, M. (2019). *Welcome to the Genome: A User's Guide to the Genetic Past, Present and Future*, 2nd ed. Hoboken: Wiley.

*Higham, T. (2021). *The World Before Us: The New Science Behind Our Human Origins*. New Haven: Yale University Press.

*Richter, D. and Wagner, G. A. (2015). Chronometric methods in paleoanthropology. In: W. Henke and I. Tattersall (eds), *Handbook of Paleoanthropology*, pp. 317–350, volume 1, 2nd ed. New York: Springer.

*Sponheimer, M. and Lee-Thorp, J. (2007). Hominin paleodiets: The contribution of stable isotopes. In: W. Henke and I. Tattersall (eds), *Handbook of Paleoanthropology*, pp. 554–585, volume 1, 2nd ed. Heidelberg: Springer.

*Weber, G. W. (2105). Virtual anthropology and biomechanics. In: W. Henke and I. Tattersall (eds), *Handbook of Paleoanthropology*, pp. 937–968, volume 1, 2nd ed. Heidelberg: Springer.

*Ungar, P. S. (2017) *Evolution's Bite: A Story of Teeth, Diet, and Human Origins*. Princeton: Princeton University Press.

Chapter 3

Ardrey, R. (1961). *African Genesis*. New York: Atheneum.

Black, D. (1931). Evidences of the use of fire by Sinanthropus. *Bulletin of the Geological Society of China* 11: 107–108.

Boule, M. (1911–1913). L'homme fossile de La Chapelle-aux-Saints. *Annales de Paléontologie* 6–8: 1–279.

Boule, M. (1937). Le Sinanthrope. *L'Anthropologie* 47: 1–22.

Broom, R. (1936). A new fossil anthropoid skull from South Africa. *Nature* 138: 486–488.

Broom, R. and Robinson, J. T. (1949). Man contemporaneous with Swartkrans ape-man. *American Journal of Physical Anthropology* 8: 151–156.

Busk, G. (1864). Pithecan priscoid man from Gibraltar. *The Reader*, July 23.

Dart, R. A. (1925). *Australopithecus africanus:* The man-ape of South Africa. *Nature* 115: 195–199.

Dart, R. A. (1957). The osteodontokeratic culture of *Australopithecus prometheus*. *Transvaal Museum Memoir* 10: 1–105.

Darwin, C. R. (1859). *On the Origin of Species by Means of Natural Selection: Or the Preservation of Favoured Races in the Struggle for Life*. London: John Murray.

Darwin, C. R. (1871). *The Descent of Man in Relation to Sex*. London: John Murray.

Dawson, C. and Woodward, A. S. (1913). On the discovery of a Palaeolithic human skull and mandible in a flint-bearing gravel overlying the Wealden (Hastings Beds) at Piltdown, Fletching, (Sussex). *Quarterly Journal of the Geological Society of London* 69: 117–151.

Dobzhansky, T. (1944). On species and races of living and fossil man. *American Journal of Physical Anthropology* 2: 251–265.

Dubois, E. (1894). Pithecanthropus erectus, *eine menschenähnliche Uebergangsform aus Java*. Batavia: Landesdruckerei.

Gregory, W. K. (1939). The South African fossil man-apes and the origin of the human dentition. *Journal of the American Dental Association* 26: 645.

Howell, F. C. (1951). The place of Neanderthal Man in human evolution. *American Journal of Physical Anthropology* 9: 379–416.

Howell, F. C. (1952). Pleistocene glacial ecology and the evolution of "Classic Neanderthal" man. *Southwestern Journal of Anthropology* 8: 377–410.

Hrdlička, A. (1927). The Neanderthal phase of man. *Journal of the Royal Anthropological Institute* 57: 249–274.

Huxley, T. H. (1863). *Evidence as to Man's Place in Nature*. London: Williams & Norgate.

Keith, A. (1915). *The Antiquity of Man*. London: Williams and Norgate.

King, W. (1863). The Neanderthal skull. *Anthropological Review* 1: 393–94.

*Le Gros Clark, W. E. (1967). *Man-Apes or Ape-Men? The Story of Discoveries in Africa*. New York: Holt, Rinehart and Winston.

Mayr, E. (1950). Taxonomic categories in fossil hominids. *Cold Spring Harbor Symposia on Quantitative Biology* 15: 109–118.

Mortillet, G. de (1883). *Le Préhistorique: Antiquité de l'Homme*. Paris: Reinwald.

Schaaffhausen, H. (1858). Zur Kentniss der ältesten Rassenschädel. [On the crania of the most ancient races of man]. *Natural History Reviews* 1: 155–176 (1861 translation, with introduction by G. Busk).]

Schwalbe, G. (1899). Studien über *Pithecanthropus erectus* Dubois. *Morphologische Anthropologie* 1: 16–228.

Schwalbe, G. (1900). *Der Neanderthalschädel. Jahrbuch der Verhandlung Altets Rheinlande* 106: 1–72.

*Spencer, F. (1990). *Piltdown: A Scientific Forgery*. London: Natural History Museum/Oxford University Press.

*Tattersall, I. (2009). *The Fossil Trail: How We Know What We Think We Know about Human Evolution*, 2nd ed. New York: Oxford University Press.

*Theunissen, B. (1988). *Eugene Dubois and the Ape-Man from Java: The History of the First "Missing Link" and Its Discoverer*. Dordrecht: Kluwer Academic.

Weidenreich, F. (1947). Facts and speculations concerning the origin of *Homo sapiens*. *American Anthropologist* 49: 187–203.

Woodward, A. S. (1921). A new cave man from Rhodesia, South Africa. *Nature* 108: 371–372.

Chapter 4

Abbate, E., Albianelli, A., Azzaroli, A., et al. (1998). A one-million-year-old *Homo* cranium from the Danakil (Afar) Depression of Eritrea. *Nature* 393: 458–460.

Alemseged, Z., Wynn, J. G., Kimbel, W. H., et al. (2005). A new hominin from the Basal Member of the Hadar Formation at Dikika, Ethiopia, and its geological context. *Journal of Human Evolution* 49: 499–514.

Arsuaga, J.-L., Martinez, I., Gracia, A., Carretero, J.-M., and Carbonell, E. (1993). Three new human skulls from the Sima de los Huesos Middle Pleistocene site in Sierra de Atapuerca, Spain. *Nature* 362: 534–537.

Asfaw, B., Gilbert, W. H., Beyene, Y., et al. (2002). Remains of *Homo erectus* from Bouri, Middle Awash, Ethiopia. *Nature* 416: 317–320.

Berger, L. R., de Ruiter, D. J., Churchill, S. E., et al. (2010). *Australopithecus sediba*: A new species of *Homo*-like australopith from South Africa. *Science* 328: 195–204.

Berger, L. R., Hawks, J., de Ruiter, D. J., et al. (2015). *Homo naledi*, a new species of the genus *Homo* from the Dinaledi Chamber, South Africa. *eLife* 2015(4): e09560.

Brace, C. L. (1964). The fate of the "Classic" Neanderthals: A consideration of hominid catastrophism. *Current Anthropology* 5: 3–43.

Brown, F., Harris, J., Leakey, R. E. F., and Walker, A. C. (1985). Early *Homo erectus* skeleton from west Lake Turkana, Kenya. *Nature* 316: 788–792.

Brown, P., Sutikna, T., Morwood, M. J. et al. (2004). A new small-bodied hominin from the Late Pleistocene of Flores, Indonesia. *Nature* 431: 1055–1061.

Brunet, M., Guy, F., Pilbeam, D., et al. (2002). A new hominid from the Upper Miocene of Chad, Central Africa. *Nature* 418: 145–151.

Cann, R. L., Stoneking, M., and Wilson, A. C. (1987). Mitochondrial DNA and human evolution. *Nature* 325: 31–36.

Conroy, G. C., Jolly, C. J., Cramer, D., and Kalb, J. E. (1978). Newly discovered fossil hominid skull from the Afar Depression, Ethiopia. *Nature* 275: 67–70.

Day, M. H., Leakey, R. E. F., Walker, A. C., and Wood, B. A. (1976). New hominids from East Turkana, Kenya. *American Journal of Physical Anthropology* 45: 369–436.

*Gibbons, A. (2006). *The First Human: The Race to Discover Our Earliest Ancestors*. New York: Doubleday.

Groves, C. P. and Mazak, V. (1975). An approach to the taxonomy of the Hominidae: Gracile Villafranchian hominids of Africa. *Casopis pro Mineralogii Geologii* 20: 225–247.

Hailie-Selassie, Y. Laimer, B. L. , Alene, M., et al. (2010). An early *Australopithecus afarensis* postcranium from Woranso-Mille, Ethiopia. *Proceedings of the National Academy of Sciences, USA* 107: 12121–12126.

Haile-Selassie, Y., Melillo, S. M., Vazzana, A., Benazzi, F., and Ryan, T. M. (2019). A 3.8-million-year-old hominin cranium from Woranso-Mille, Ethiopia. *Nature* 573, 214–219.

*Harcourt-Smith, W. E. H. (2015). The origins of bipedal locomotion. In: W. Henke and I. Tattersall (eds), *Handbook of Paleoanthropology*, pp. 1919–1960, volume 3, 2nd ed. New York: Springer.

Howell, F. C. (1978). Hominidae. In: V. J. Maglio and H. B. S. Cooke (eds), *Evolution of African Mammals*, pp. 154–248. Cambridge, MA: Harvard University Press.

Isaac, G. L. (1978). The food-sharing behavior of proto-human hominids. *Scientific American* 238: 90–108.

Johanson, D. C. (ed.) (1982). Pliocene hominid fossils from Hadar, Ethiopia. *American Journal of Physical Anthropology* 57(4): 373–724.

Johanson, D. C. and White, T. D. (1979). A systematic assessment of early African hominids. *Science* 202: 321–330.

Johanson, D. C., White, T. D., and Coppens, Y. (1978). A new species of the genus *Australopithecus* (Primates: Hominidae) from the Pliocene of eastern Africa. *Kirtlandia* 28: 1–14.

*Johanson, D. J. and Edey, M. A. (1981). *Lucy: The Beginnings of Humankind*. New York: Simon and Schuster.

Harmand, S., Lewis, J., Feibel, C., et al. (2015). 3.3-million-year-old stone tools from Lomekwi 3, West Turkana, Kenya. *Nature* 521: 310–315.

Hublin, J.-J., Sirakov, N., Aldeias, V., et al. (2020). Initial Upper Palaeolithic *Homo sapiens* from Bacho Kiro Cave, Bulgaria. *Nature* 581: 299–302.

*Kalb, J. (2001). *Adventures in the Bone Trade: The Race to Discover Human Ancestors in Ethiopia's Afar Depression*. New York: Copernicus Books.

Kimbel, W. H., Johanson, D. C., and Rak, Y. (1997). Systematic assessment of a maxilla of *Homo* from Hadar, Ethiopia. *American Journal of Physical Anthropology* 103: 235–262.

*Kimbel, W. H., Rak, Y., and Johanson, D. C. (2004). *The Skull of* Australopithecus afarensis. New York: Oxford University Press.

Krings, M., Geisert, H., Schmitz, R. W., Krainitzki, H., and Pääbo, S. (1999). DNA sequence of the mitochondrial hypervariable region II from the Neandertal type specimen. *Proceedings of the National Academy of Sciences, USA* 96: 5581–5585.

Leakey, L. S. B. (1959). A new fossil skull from Olduvai. *Nature* 184: 491–493.

Leakey, L. S. B., Evernden, J. F., and Curtis, G. H. (1961). Age of Bed I, Olduvai Gorge, Tanganyika. *Nature* 191: 478–479.

Leakey, L. S. B., Tobias, P. V., and Napier, J. R. (1964). A new species of the genus *Homo* from Olduvai Gorge. *Nature* 202: 7–10.

Leakey, M. D. (1966). A review of the Oldowan culture from Olduvai Gorge, Tanzania. *Nature* 210: 462–466.

*Leakey, M. D. and Harris J. M. (eds) (1987). *Laetoli: A Pliocene Site in Northern Tanzania*. Oxford: Clarendon Press.

Leakey, M. G., Feibel, C. S., McDougall, I., Ward, C., and Walker, A. C. (1995). New four-million-year-old hominid species from Kanapoi and Allia Bay, Kenya. *Nature* 376: 565–571.

Leakey, M. G., Spoor, F. Brown, F. H., et al. (2001). New hominin genus from eastern Africa shows diverse middle Pliocene lineages. *Nature* 410: 433–440.

Leakey, R. E. F. (1970). New hominid remains and early artefacts from Northern Kenya. *Nature* 226: 226–228.

Leakey, R. E. F. (1971). Further evidence of Lower Pleistocene hominids from East Rudolf, Kenya. *Nature* 231: 241–245.

Leakey, R. E. F. and Walker, A. C. (1976). *Australopithecus, Homo erectus* and the single species hypothesis. *Nature* 261: 572–574.

*Lewin, R. (1987). *Bones of Contention: Controversies in the Search for Human Origins*. New York: Simon and Schuster.

Lordkipanidze, D., Jashashvili, T., Vekua, A., et al. (2007). Postcranial evidence from early *Homo* from Dmanisi, Georgia. *Nature* 449: 305–310.

Lumley, M.-A. de and Lordkipanidze, D. (2006). L'homme de Dmanissi (*Homo georgicus*), il y a 1 810 000 ans. *Paléontologie humaine et Préhistoire* 5: 273–281.

Macchiarelli, R., Bondioli, L. , Chech, M. , et al. (2004). The Late Early Pleistocene human remains from Buia, Danakil Depression, Eritrea. *Rivista Italiana di Paleontologia e Stratigrafia* 110: 133–144.

McPherron, S., Alemseged, Z., Marean, C., et al. (2010). Evidence for stone-tool-assisted consumption of animal tissues before 3.39 million years ago at Dikika, Ethiopia. *Nature* 466: 857–860.

*Pääbo, S. (2014). *Neanderthal Man: In Search of Lost Genomes*. New York: Basic Books.

*Reader, J. (1981). *Missing Links: The Hunt for Earliest Man*. Boston: Little, Brown.

Rightmire, G. P., Lordkipanidze, D., and Vekua, A. (2006). Anatomical descriptions, comparative studies, and evolutionary significance of the hominin skulls from Dmanisi, Republic of Georgia. *Journal of Human Evolution* 50: 115–141.

Senut, B., Pickford, M. Gommery, D., et al. (2001). First hominid from the Miocene (Lukeino Formation, Kenya). *Earth and Planetary Sciences* 332: 137–144.

*Tattersall, I. (2009). *The Fossil Trail: How We Know What We Think We Know about Human Evolution*, 2nd ed. New York: Oxford University Press.

Tobias, P. V., and G. H. R. von Koenigswald. (1964). Comparison between the Olduvai hominines and those of Java and some implications for hominid phylogeny. *Nature* 204: 515–518.

Tocheri, M. W., Orr, C. M., Larson, S. G., et al. (2007). The primitive wrist of *Homo floresiensis* and its implications for hominin evolution. *Science* 317: 1743–1745.

Walker, A. C. and Leakey, R. (1993). *The Nariokotome* Homo erectus *skeleton*. Cambridge, MA: Harvard University Press.

White, T. Suwa, D. G., and Asfaw, B. (1994). *Australopithecus ramidus*, a new species of early hominid from Aramis, Ethiopia. *Nature* 371: 306–312.

White, T. D., Asfaw, B., DeGusta, D., et al. (2003). Pleistocene *Homo sapiens* from Middle Awash, Ethiopia. *Nature* 423: 742–747.

Wolpoff, M. H., Wu, X., and Thorne, A. G. (1984). Modern *Homo sapiens* origins: A general theory of hominid evolution involving evidence from East Asia. In: F. H. Smith and F. Spencer (eds), *The Origins of Modern Humans: A World Survey of the Fossil Evidence*, pp. 411–483. New York: Alan R. Liss

*Wood, B. (1991). *Koobi Fora Research Project, Vol. 4: Hominid Cranial Remains*. Oxford: Clarendon Press.

Wood, B. (1992). Origin and evolution of the genus *Homo*. *Nature*, 355: 783–790.

Wood, B. and Collard, M. (1999). The human genus. *Science* 284: 65–71.

Zwir, I., Del-Val, C., Hintsanen, M., et al. (2021). Evolution of genetic networks for human creativity. *Molecular Psychiatry*. https://doi.org.10.1038/s41380-021–01097-y.

Chapter 5

Boehme, M. (2020). *Ancient Bones: Unearthing the Astonishing New Story of How We Became Human*. Vancouver: Greystone Books.

Brunet, M., Guy, F., Pilbeam, D., et al. (2002). A new hominid from the Upper Miocene of Chad, Central Africa. *Nature* 418: 145–151.

Darwin, C. (1871). *The Descent of Man, and Selection in Relation to Sex*. London: John Murray.

Haile-Selassie, Y., Melillo, S. M., Vazzana, A., Benazzi, F., and Ryan, T. M. (2019). A 3.8-million-year-old hominin cranium from Woranso-Mille, Ethiopia. *Nature* 573, 214–219.

*Harcourt-Smith, W. E. H. (2015). The origins of bipedal locomotion. In: W. Henke and I. Tattersall (eds), *Handbook of Paleoanthropology*, pp. 1919–1960, volume 3, 2nd ed. New York: Springer.

Harmand, S., Lewis, J., Feibel, C., et al. (2015). 3.3-million-year-old stone tools from Lomekwi 3, West Turkana, Kenya. *Nature* 521: 310–315.

Hart, D. and Sussman, R. W. (2009). *Man the Hunted: Primates, Predators, and Human Evolution*. Boulder: Westview Press.

Heinzelin, J. de, Clark, J. D. , White, T. , et al. (1999). Environment and behavior of 2.5-million-year-old Bouri hominids. *Science* 284: 625–629.

Johanson, D. et al. (1982). Special Issue: Pliocene hominid fossils from Hadar, Ethiopia. *American Journal of Physical Anthropology* 57(4): 373–724.

Kappelman, J., Ketcham, R., Pearce, S., et al. (2016). Perimortem fractures in Lucy suggest mortality from fall out of tall tree. *Nature* 537: 503–507.

Köhler, M. and Moyà-Solà, S. (1997). Ape-like or hominid-like? The positional behavior of *Oreopithecus bambolii* reconsidered. *Proceedings of the National Academy of Science, USA* 94(21): 11747–11750.

Leakey, M. G., Feibel, C. S., McDougall, I., Ward, C., and Walker, A. C. (1995). New four-million-year-old hominid species from Kanapoi and Allia Bay, Kenya. *Nature* 376: 565–571.

McPherron, S., Alemseged, Z., Marean, C., et al. (2010). Evidence for stone-tool-assisted consumption of animal tissues before 3.39 million years ago at Dikika, Ethiopia. *Nature* 466: 857–860.

Pruetz, J. D. and Bertolani, P. (2007). Savanna chimpanzees, *Pan troglodytes verus*, hunt with tools. *Current Biology* 17: 412–417.

*Stern, J. T. (2000). Climbing to the top: A personal memoir of *Australopithecus afarensis*. *Evolutionary Anthropology* 9(3): 113–133.

*Tattersall, I. (2016). Prerequisites for hominid bipedality. In: F. Ribot Trafí (ed.), *Homenaje al Dr. José Gibert Clols. Una vida dedicada a la ciencia y al* *conocimiento de los primeros europeos*, pp. 83–91. Granada: Publicaciones Diputación de Granada.

*Tomasello, M. and Herrmann, E. (2010). Ape and human cognition: What's the difference? *Current Directions in Psychological Science* 19(1). https://doi.org/10.1177/0963721409359300.

White, T. D., Suwa, G., and Asfaw, B. (1994). *Australopithecus ramidus*, a new species of early hominid from Aramis, Ethiopia. *Nature* 371: 306–312.

White, T. D., Suwa, G., and Asfaw, B. (1995). Corrigendum: *Australopithecus ramidus*, a new species of early hominid from Aramis, Ethiopia. *Nature* 375: 88.

White, T. D. , et al. (2009). Special Issue on *Ardipithecus ramidus*. *Science* 326 (5949): 5–106.

Wynn, J. G., Sponheimer, M., Kimbel, W. H., et al. (2013). Diet of *Australopithecus afarensis* from the Pliocene Hadar Formation, Ethiopia. *Proceedings of the National Academy of Sciences, USA* 110: 10495–10500.

Zollikofer, C., Ponce de León, M. , Lieberman, D. , et al. (2005). Virtual cranial reconstruction of *Sahelanthropus tchadensis*. *Nature* 434: 755–759.

Chapter 6

Aiello, L. and Wheeler, P. (1995). The expensive-tissue hypothesis: The brain and the digestive system in human and primate evolution. *Current Anthropology* 36: 199–212.

Berger, L. R., de Ruiter, D. J., Churchill, S. E., et al. (2010). *Australopithecus sediba*: A new species of *Homo*-like australopith from South Africa. *Science* 328: 195–204.

Cunningham, D. L., Graves, R. R., Westcott, D. J., and McCarthy, R. C. (2018). The effect of ontogeny on estimates of KNM-WT 15000's adult body size. *Journal of Human Evolution* 121: 119–127.

Gabunia, L., Vekua, A., Lordkipanidze, D., et al. (2000). Earliest Pleistocene hominid cranial remains from Dmanisi, Republic of Georgia: Taxonomy, geological setting, and age. *Science* 288: 1019–1025.

Graves, R. R., Lupo, A. C., McCarthy, R. C., Wescott, D. J., and Cunningham, D. L. (2010). Just how strapping was KNM-WT 15000? *Journal of Human Evolution* 59: 542–554

Lordkipanidze, D., Jashashvili, T., Vekua, A., et al. (2007). Postcranial evidence from early *Homo* from Dmanisi, Georgia. *Nature* 449: 305–310.

Lordkipanidze, D., Ponce de León, M. S., Margvelashvili, A., et al. (2013). A complete skull from Dmanisi, Georgia, and the evolutionary biology of early *Homo*. *Science* 342: 326–331.

Matsu'ura, S., Kondo, M., Danhara, Y., et al. (2020). Age control of the first appearance datum for Javanese *Homo erectus* in the Sangiran area. *Science* 367: 210–214.

Rizal, Y., Westaway, K. E., Zaim, Y., et al. (2020). Last appearance of *Homo erectus* at Ngandong, Java, 117,000–108,00 years ago. *Nature* 577: 381–385.

Ruxton, G. and Wilkinson, D. M. (2012). Endurance running and its relevance to scavenging by early hominins. *Evolution* 67: 861–867.

Schwartz, J. H. and Tattersall, I. (2000). What constitutes *Homo erectus*? *Acta Anthropologica Sinica* 19: 21–25.

Schwartz, J. H., Tattersall, I., and Zhang. C. (2014). Comment on "A complete skull from Dmanisi, Georgia, and the evolutionary biology of early *Homo*." *Science* 344: 360-a.

*Tattersall, I. (2015). *Homo ergaster* and its contemporaries. In: W. Henke and I. Tattersall (eds), *Handbook of Paleoanthropology*, pp. 2167–2188, volume 3, 2nd ed. Heidelberg: Springer.

Tattersall, I. (2017). Species, genera, and phylogenetic structure in the human fossil record: A modest proposal. *Evolutionary Anthropology* 26: 116–118.

Villmoare, B., Kimbel, W. H., Seyoum, C., et al. (2015). Early *Homo* at 2.8 Ma from Ledi-Geraru, Afar, Ethiopia. *Science* 347: 1352–1355.

Walker, A. C. and Leakey, R. (1993). *The Nariokotome* Homo erectus *skeleton*. Cambridge, MA: Harvard University Press.

Wheeler, P. (1991). The thermoregulatory advantages of hominid bipedalism in open equatorial environments: The contribution of increased convective heat loss and cutaneous evaporative cooling. *Journal of Human Evolution* 21: 107–115.

*Wood, B. (1991). *Koobi Fora Research Project, vol. 4: Hominid Cranial Remains*. Oxford: Clarendon Press.

Wrangham, R. (2009). *Catching Fire: How Cooking Made Us Human*. New York: Basic Books.

Chapter 7

Bocherens, H., Drucker, G., Billiou, D., Patou-Mathis, M. and Vandermeersch, B. (2005). Isotopic evidence for diet and subsistence pattern of the Saint-Césaire I Neanderthal: Review and use of a multi-source mixing model. *Journal of Human Evolution* 49: 71–87.

Duveau, J., Berillon, G., Verna, C., Laisné, G., and Cliquet, D. (2019). The composition of a Neandertal social group revealed by the hominin footprints at Le Rozel (Normandy, France). *Proceedings of the National Academy of Sciences, USA* 116: 19409–19414.

Hoffmann, D. L., Standish, C. D., Garcia-Diez, M., et al. (2018). U-Th dating of carbonate crusts reveals Neandertal origin of Iberian cave art. *Science* 359: 912–915

Higham, T., Douka, K., Wood, R., et al. (2014). The timing and spatiotemporal patterning of Neanderthal disappearance. *Nature* 512: 306–309.

Hublin, J. J., Sirakov, N., Aldeias, V., et al. (2020). Initial Upper Palaeolithic *Homo sapiens* from Bacho Kiro Cave, Bulgaria. *Nature* 581: 299–302.

Jaubert, J., Verheyden, S., Genty, D., et al. (2016). Early Neanderthal constructions deep in Bruniquel Cave in southwestern France. *Nature* 434: 111–115.

Joordens, J., d'Errico, F. , Wesselingh, F. , et al. (2015). *Homo erectus* at Trinil on Java used shells for tool production and engraving. *Nature* 518: 228–231.

Lalueza-Fox, C., Rosas, A., Estalrrich, A., et al. (2011). Genetic evidence for patrilocal mating behavior among Neandertal groups. *Proceedings of the National Academy of Sciences, USA* 108: 250–253.

*Lombard, M. (2012). Thinking through the Middle Stone Age of sub-Saharan Africa. *Quaternary International* 270: 140–155.

Mayoral, E., Díaz-Martínez, I., Duveau, J., et al. (2021). Tracking late Pleistocene Neandertals on the Iberian coast. *Scientific Reports* 11: 4103.

Meyer, M., Arsuaga, J. L., de Filippo, C., et al. (2016). Nuclear DNA sequences from the Middle Pleistocene Sima de los Huesos hominins. *Nature* 531: 504–507.

Pearce, E., Stringer, C., and Dunbar, R. I. M. (2013). New insights into differences in brain organization between Neanderthals and anatomically modern humans. *Proceedings of the Royal Society B* 280: 20130168.

Ponce de León, M. S. and Zollikofer, C. P. E. (2001). Neandertal cranial ontogeny and its implications for late hominid diversity. *Nature* 412: 534–538.

Radovčić, D., Sršen, A. O., Radovčić, J., and Frayer, D. W. (2015). Evidence for Neandertal jewelry: Modified white-tailed eagle claws at Krapina. *PLoS One* 10(3): e0119802.

Sawyer, S., Renauda, G., Viola, B., et al. (2015). Nuclear and mitochondrial DNA sequences from two Denisovan individuals. *Proceedings of the National Academy of Sciences, USA* 112: 15696–15700.

Slimak, L., Fietzke, J., Geneste, J.-M., and Ontanon, R. (2018). Comment on "U-Th dating of carbonate crusts reveals Neandertal origin of Iberian cave art." *Science* 361: eaau1371.

Slon, V., Hopfe, C., Weiss, C. L., et al. (2017). Neandertal and Denisovan DNA from Pleistocene sediments. *Science* 356: 605–608.

*Sykes, R. W. (2020). *Kindred: Neanderthal Life, Love, Death and Art*. London: Bloomsbury Sigma.

Thieme, H. (1997). Lower Palaeolithic hunting spears from Germany. *Nature* 385: 807–810.

Weyrich, L. S., Duchene, S., Soubrier, J., et al. (2017). Neandertal behaviour, diet, and disease inferred using ancient DNA preserved in dental calculus. *Nature* 544: 357–361.

Zwir, I., Del-Val, C., Hintsanen, M., et al. (2021). Evolution of genetic networks for human creativity. *Molecular Psychiatry*. https://doi.org.10.1038/s41380-021-0 1097-y.

Chapter 8

Aubert, M., Brumm, A., Ramli, M., et al. (2014). Pleistocene cave art from Sulawesi, Indonesia. *Nature* 514: 223–227.

Aubert, M., Setiawan, P., Oktaviana, A., et al. (2018). Palaeolithic cave art in Borneo. *Nature* 564: 254–257.

Aubert, M., Lebe, R., Oktaviana, A. A., et al. (2019). Earliest hunting scene in prehistoric art. *Nature* 576: 442–445.

*Balter, M. (2011). Was North Africa the launch pad for modern human migrations? *Science* 331: 20–23.

Berwick, R. C. and Chomsky, N. (2016). *Why Only Us: Language and Evolution*. Cambridge, MA: MIT Press.

Bouzouggar, A., Barton, N., Vanhaeren, M., et al. (2007). 82,000-year-old shell beads from North Africa and implications for the origins of modern human behavior. *Proceedings of the National Academy of Sciences, USA* 104: 9964–9969.

Brown, K. S., Marean, C. W., Herries, A. I.R., et al. (2009). Fire as an engineering tool of early modern humans. *Science* 325: 859–862.

Fu, Q., Posth, C., Hadjdinjak, M., et al. (2016). The genetic history of Ice Age Europe. *Nature* 534: 200–204.

Hadjdinjak, M., Mafessoni, F., Skov, L., et al. (2021). Initial Palaeolithic humans in Europe had recent Neanderthal ancestry. *Nature* 592: 253–257.

Henshilwood, C. S. , d'Errico, F. , Vanhaeren, M. , van Niekerk, K. , and Jacobs, Z. (2004). Middle Stone Age shell beads from South Africa. *Science* 303: 404–407.

Henshilwood, C. S., d'Errico, F. , and Watts, I. (2009). Engraved ochres from the Middle Stone Age levels at Blombos Cave, South Africa. *Journal of Human Evolution* 57: 27–47.

Henshilwood, C. S. , d'Errico, F. , van Niekerk, K. , et al. (2011). A 100,000-year-old ochre-processing workshop at Blombos Cave, South Africa. *Science* 334: 219–222.

McDougall, I., Brown, F. H., and Fleagle, J. G. (2005). Stratigraphic placement and age of modern humans from Kibish, Ethiopia. *Nature* 433, 733–736.

Posth, C., Renaud, G., Mittnik, A., et al. (2016). Pleistocene mitochondrial genomes suggest a single major dispersal of non-Africans and a late glacial population turnover in Europe. *Current Biology* 26: 827–833.

Rasmussen, M., Guo, X., Wang, Y., et al. (2011). An aboriginal Australian genome reveals separate human dispersals into Asia. *Science* 334: 94–98.

*Reich, D. (2018). *Who We Are and How We Got Here: Ancient DNA and the New Science of the Human Past*. New York: Vintage Books.

Rito, T., Vieira, D., Silva, M., et al. (2019). A dispersal of *Homo sapiens* from southern to eastern Africa immediately preceded the out-of-Africa migration. *Scientific Reports* 9: 4728

*Schwartz, J. H. and Tattersall, I. (2010). Fossil evidence for the origin of *Homo sapiens*. *Yearbook of Physical Anthropology* 53: 94–121.

*Stringer, C. (2016). The origin and evolution of *Homo sapiens*. *Philosophical Transactions of the Royal Society B* 371: 20150237.

Tattersall, I. (2018). Brain size and the emergence of modern human cognition. In: J. H. Schwartz (ed.), *Rethinking Human Evolution*. Cambridge, MA: MIT Press, pp. 319–334.

Tattersall, I. (2019). The Minimalist Program and the origin of language: A view from paleoanthropology. *Frontiers in Psychology* 10: 677. https://doi.org/10.3389/fpsyg.2019.00677

Wadley, L. (2012). Two "moments in time" during Middle Stone Age occupations of Sibudu, South Africa. *Southern African Humanities* 24: 79–97.

White, T. D., Asfaw, B., DeGusta, D., et al. (2003). Pleistocene *Homo sapiens* from Middle Awash, Ethiopia. *Nature* 423: 742–747.

Willerslev, E. and Meltzer, D. J. (2021). Peopling of the Americas as inferred from ancient genomics. *Nature* 594: 356–364.

Yang, M. A., Fan, X., Sun, B., et al. (2020). Ancient DNA indicates human population shifts and admixture in northern and southern China. *Science* 369: 282–288.

Figure Credits

6.1   Artwork by Don McGranaghan.
6.2   Artwork by Nick Amorosi.
7.1   Artwork by Don McGranaghan.
7.2   Artwork by Diana Salles, after a concept by Henry de Lumley.
7.3   Artwork by Patricia Wynne.
7.4   Artwork by Patricia Wynne (Sima) and Don McGranaghan (Steinheim).
7.5   Artwork by Don McGranaghan.
8.1   Artwork by Don McGranaghan.
8.2   Artwork by Jennifer Steffey, after a photo by Ken Mowbray of a reconstruction by Gary Sawyer and Blaine Maley.
8.3   Artwork by Patricia Wynne (Herto) and Don McGranaghan (Ngaloba, Ndutu).
8.4   Artwork by Patricia Wynne.
8.5   Artwork by Diana Salles.

Index

Index: references to figures are in **bold**; to tables in *italics*

Printed in the United States
by Baker & Taylor Publisher Services